ASPECTS OF THE DEPRESSION

ASPECTS OF
THE DEPRESSION

EDITED BY

FELIX MORLEY

*Chairman, Committee on Economics, The National
Advisory Council on Radio in Education*

Essay Index Reprint Series

Originally published by:

THE UNIVERSITY OF CHICAGO PRESS

BOOKS FOR LIBRARIES PRESS

FREEPORT, NEW YORK

First Published 1932
Reprinted 1968

LIBRARY OF CONGRESS CATALOG CARD NUMBER:
68-22932

PRINTED IN THE UNITED STATES OF AMERICA

PREFACE

I T IS comparatively easy for the educational broadcaster to assemble a list of speakers and to bring them to the microphone. A fundamental error that has been made by the educational broadcaster in America is that too often he has regarded the mere transference of the classroom to the air as education. Of course it is, but only in a somewhat limited sense. It is the sort of education that would result if a college should engage a teacher, assign a schedule, neglect to announce the hour or place his class would meet, fail to send out catalogues to students, disregard assigning required texts or collateral reading—in short, abandon any plan of guidance.

When the National Advisory Council on Radio in Education was far enough along in its very brief existence to regard seriously the broadcasting of programs which would be offered under its auspices by recognized leaders in subjects of public concern and interest, a decision was made to attempt every sort of aid to the listener, both before and after the broadcast. There was little to guide the Council. A project of this kind had never before been tried on a nation-wide basis. There were no precedents. No mistakes had been made from which we could profit.

(v)

There were no successes for us to emulate. The obvious thing for us to do was to decide what we, in our well-meaning inexperience, felt was desirable and sound from a common-sense standpoint. So we —and by "we" is meant the energetic and wise committees which are responsible for Council programs, as well as the members of the Council staff— decided that several basic things were absolutely necessary.

First we had to assemble the audience for these radio addresses. That, we felt, required dignified and country-wide publicity. In the next place we decided that it was essential to have a guide for the listener, a sort of track for his listening to run on during the series. All of us believed very sincerely that the chief value in broadcasts of this sort is their stimulative effect. Then, with the help of the American Library Association we planned to compile reading lists which would give an active mind a chance to roam all over the subject so that he could either follow it generally or select one little corner of it where he could browse to his heart's content. Finally, realizing that a broadcast, per se, is an ephemeral thing at best, we made arrangements to put our program, so far as possible, into more enduring printed form.

It is unnecessary to indicate how the Council proceeded to develop each of these phases of what it regarded as its minimum responsibility. It is sufficient to point out that this volume is the permanent record of the Council's broadcasts on "Economic Aspects of the Depression" in the first series devised by our Council Committee on Economics, appointed on recommendations made by the American Economic Association, the League for Industrial Democracy, and the Brookings Institution. This Committee has worked long and faithfully on the details of planning and producing this very successful series, and Felix Morley was its guiding genius. The programs were broadcast once a week for thirty-two weeks over a country-wide network of the National Broadcasting Company, from October 17, 1931 to May 21, 1932. Starting with a chain of about forty stations this network had grown to a total of fifty-five stations when the series ended.

It is impossible to determine how successful the venture has been. That it has been well received there is no doubt, for the correspondence which has resulted is a clear indication of that fact. That it could have been more successful no one realizes more firmly than the same "we" who have been so close to it from the beginning. We know where the machinery has creaked. We know where what we planned fell short of expectations. We know where our greatest satisfactions lie. We are convinced that all of it has been worth while and modestly feel that a judicial appraisal of success and disappointment will result in a very favorable balance. With this thought in mind we have no hesitation whatsoever in offering to the public in permanent form a record which we think has a distinct place in the literature of radio and in the literature of economics as well.

In attempting to determine what subject the Council should present to the public as it embarked upon its early experiment in broadcasting, it was inevitable that the depression and all its economic phases should be considered—and selected. As President Butler stated so aptly in his introductory address,

Economics, which has interested reflective man since the time of Aristotle, has from the beginning of time played a large and often controlling part in the development of civilization and of social and political institutions on this earth. It has never been so important as it is at this moment. The center of gravity of dominant human interest has everywhere shifted from questions and problems that are primarily political to questions and problems that are primarily economic. For several centuries the Western world of Europe and of America was concerned in working out political institutions, in discovering and applying political principles which would give opportunity for the achievement of their dominant political ideals. These may all be summed up in the single word "liberty." Men were in search of civil, political, and religious liberty; and for generation after generation they exerted themselves now here, now there, to break down those systems of monarchial or group control which put restrictions upon liberty. So it was that the English, the French, and the American revolutions came to pass and wrote on history's page the vitally important lessons which they teach and record.

For at least one hundred years, however, questions of pure politics, questions of how government should be organized, questions of how authority should be distributed, have grown less and less significant, for human interest has passed over to the field of economics. Men are everywhere now insisting that political institutions, whatever they may be, shall be so worked, so applied, so altered if need be, that the production, the just distribution, and the enjoyment of the world's wealth by the whole population shall be advanced. The kind of argument by which the English, the French, and the American revolutions were explained and defended is no longer heard. The new kind of argument which most engages public interest and attention starts from an economic base and travels by an economic road toward an economic goal. "Socialism" and "communism," two words which were quite unknown a hundred years ago, are now on every tongue in every land, for the reason that they represent zealous and strongly supported forms of this argument.

Few things, if any, are more needed by the American people, in last resort responsible for the policies of their government, as well as for either the protection or the overthrow of their social and political systems, than an insight into the fundamental principles of economics and some understanding of the significance of prevailing economic arguments.

It will not do to shut one's eyes and ears to what is going on and let happen what will. The risk is far too great for that. What is needed is open-minded study and reflection, larger understanding, and conscious choice of policy and of purpose.

The distinguished men and women who are to present, week after week, to the American public over this radio system various aspects of these economic questions, speak with high authority. They are teachers and guides of opinion to whom we owe it to ourselves and our public responsibility to listen. From what they shall say I venture to predict very large results, not only from hearing what is said over this radio system, but from the reflection, the reading, and the discussion which that hearing will stimulate.

PREFACE

In conformity with this challenging purpose and hope, the Council welcomes the enterprise of its publishers in making available to the public this collected series of notable broadcasts, unique in the history of American radio.

LEVERING TYSON

NEW YORK
May 25, 1932

(x)

CONTENTS

ECONOMIC ASPECTS OF THE DEPRESSION

ROADS TO ECONOMIC RECOVERY

(xi)

CONTENTS

NEW SOCIAL RESPONSIBILITIES

ECONOMIC ASPECTS OF THE DEPRESSION

FORERUNNERS OF THE PRESENT DEPRESSION

Ernest L. Bogart

THE other day an acquaintance stopped me on the street and asked if I thought that we would never recover from the present depression but would have to adjust ourselves permanently to conditions of lowered production and of chronic unemployment. A banker said to me recently that the present crisis is the worst in our history and prophesied that it would probably take thirty years to restore prosperity. It may be, as our richest citizen has asserted, that "history is bunk," but a slight knowledge of our own economic development would have saved these gentlemen from much foolish talk. Indeed, one can derive a great deal of comfort from a study of the past, for the United States in the last hundred years has experienced some fifteen well-marked crises, from each of which the country has emerged, after a period of depression varying from a few months to five years, stronger and more prosperous than ever. While history never absolutely repeats itself, even a brief survey of some

(3)

of the more important crises of the past will throw needed light upon our present plight. For this purpose I shall select those of 1837, 1873, and 1893, since these were the most serious and were followed by the longest depressions.

Within the last twenty years the term "business cycle" has come into general use to describe these recurrent circles of good times, speculation, and depression, and it is to this cycle that I wish to direct your attention. In every case we have gone ahead too fast in the investment of capital in fixed forms, far in advance of the immediate needs of the country, and then have been compelled to pause and catch our breath.

The crisis of 1837 was preceded by the construction on a large scale of internal improvements in the form of turnpikes, steamboats, canals, and banks, which were designed to connect the vast region between the Appalachian Mountains and the Atlantic seaboard, to open up new markets both for the western farmer and for the eastern manufacturer, and to provide credit facilities for larger domestic trade. Difficult as it is for us to realize today, the opening of the Erie Canal was more immediately revolutionary than were the later railroad or automobile developments. Its effect on domestic commerce was phenomenal. Freight rates between New York and Buffalo were cut to one-tenth the former figure and the time for the trip was shortened from twenty to eight days.

(4)

A stream of settlers and freight began to move into the Ohio Valley, and a return movement of western produce flowed to the Atlantic coast cities. The South, too, prospered; she bought food and other supplies from the western farmers, and manufactures from eastern merchants, to whom she sold her expanding cotton production. All sections of the country shared in the new prosperity which was introduced by the revolutionary changes in transportation. It seemed as if the key to unbounded wealth had been found.

The response of the people was immediate and unmistakable. With one accord they gave themselves to speculation. It was a period of rapid change, of great economic development, and of unbounded optimism. A network of canals, 4,500 miles in all, was built—far more than the traffic could support. Steamboats multiplied in number on the Mississippi River and the Great Lakes, and throughout the West and South hundreds of private and state banks were chartered to provide the credit facilities for the expected expansion. Within a decade perhaps half a billion dollars had been invested in internal improvements, much of which was borrowed from Europe. The inflation of the currency caused higher prices, and the "new era" of good times was hailed as permanent.

In 1837 this period of expansion and speculation came to an end. The premature investments could not earn their interest charges. Depression in England curtailed the foreign demand for cotton, and in March several of the greatest cotton factors in New Orleans failed. Cotton fell from twenty cents a pound to ten. In New York 130 firms had failed by the middle of April. In May every bank in the United States suspended specie payments. Over six hundred banks failed, the discredited bank notes depreciated in value, and prices shrank to a hard-money level. When foreign investors asked for the repayment of their loans, some of the states repudiated their bonds and others delayed their interest payments. Several of the western states declared a moratorium on private debts. The government revenues fell off and Congress, called in extra session, voted $10,000,000 in Treasury notes to meet the emergency.

The crisis of 1837 was followed by a prolonged depression. Factories and workshops, organized on a boom basis, closed when the demand fell off. Thousands of operatives were discharged, and the cities were filled with the unemployed. Poorhouses everywhere were crowded. Several commission houses were broken into by the unemployed, and the food riots were ended only by the promise of the merchants to give flour to the poor. It was estimated that nine-tenths of all the eastern factories were closed, while the reduction in the number of clerks in mercantile establishments and banks still further swelled the group of the unemployed.

This crisis of 1837 was one of the most severe and

far-reaching in our history, and the depression did not come to an end until 1842. By that time, however, the effects of the earlier excesses had been overcome, weak institutions had been weeded out, and the necessary readjustments to new conditions of transportation and trade effected. Upon the firm foundation thus laid the natural buoyancy of the people soon built up a more enduring structure of prosperity than any the country had yet seen. So great was the economic development that the fifteen-year period after 1842 has usually been referred to as the "golden age" of our history.

The crisis of 1873 was the result of a too rapid and too uneven expansion. This time there was an overinvestment in farms and railroads. The Homestead Act, which gave to each settler a free farm of 160 acres, proved an irresistible attraction and drew thousands of farmers onto the western plains. These pioneers, anxious to improve their new farms, borrowed from eastern capitalists, mortgaging their lands to them. But many of them borrowed for equipment and improvement more than their farms could earn, and they frequently defaulted on interest and principal. For years "a Kansas mortgage" was a synonym for an unprofitable investment.

Even larger amounts of capital were invested in railroads, which were often built in advance of traffic and beyond the frontier of settlement. Between 1865 and 1873 the railway mileage was doubled. It is difficult today to understand how the builders could have hoped that these railways would develop traffic or earn expenses.

In the cities, factories, docks, and buildings were being constructed on an unprecedented scale. There was in all these ways an enormous absorption of circulating capital in fixed forms, many of which were not immediately remunerative. The equipment for future production along certain lines was increasing at a more rapid rate than the demand. It has been estimated that in the eight years preceding 1873 the capital invested in the United States was equal to the cost of the Civil War.

Not only was much of this expansion unwise and premature, but it was unfortunately attended by fraudulent practices. These were the days of Erie and *Credit Mobilier*, of the "salary grab" law by Congress, of whiskey frauds, of the infamous Tweed ring, and of other scandals. It was a period of unbridled individualism and of great opportunity, in which speculative excesses were restrained neither by an informed public opinion nor by a high business morality. Waste and extravagance, stimulated by an inflated currency, were seen on every hand. Conservatism in business and economy in private expenditure were disregarded in favor of so-called progressive methods. It was at this time that the phrase "frenzied finance" was added to the American vocabulary.

In September, 1873, the bubble of speculative enterprise and inflated credit burst, and a severe crisis occurred. The immediate occasion of the crash was the failure of the banking house of Jay Cooke and Company, which was heavily involved in the financing of the Northern Pacific Railroad, but an end must soon have come to the speculative expansion in any case. The news of the failure precipitated a panic in Wall Street. Securities were dumped on the market in large amounts and sold for what they would bring. Prices fell disastrously and many brokerage houses and banks failed. The Stock Exchange closed for ten days. A run on the banks started and the eastern banks suspended specie payments for forty days. Commodity prices fell, but buying power fell faster. In the single year 1873 over five thousand failures occurred with liabilities of $250,000,000. Factories, furnaces, and mills shut down, railroad building stopped, business houses were closed, and three million men were thrown out of work. A depression ensued which lasted for half a decade.

The inevitable period of liquidation and readjustment was severe and protracted. By the end of 1875 railroads had defaulted on $750,000,000 worth of bonds. A cut of 10 per cent in railway wages in 1877 was followed by strikes, riotous outbreaks, and the destruction of property. It was estimated in October of that year that in the previous twenty months there had been a shrinkage of 25 per cent in the capital employed in mercantile business.

By 1878, however, the depression had run its

course, the necessary liquidation had been completed, and the country had entered upon a new period of prosperity. The great investment in railroads and other property improvements, premature though they were, had furnished the country with excellent transportation facilities and industrial plants, and these now contributed to the production of new wealth. After 1879 the standard of living was raised, without straining the resources of the country, to levels which would have been regarded as extravagant and wasteful in 1873.

In describing the crisis of 1893 it is scarcely necessary to recount the now familiar cycle of good times, overexpansion, panic, and depression. I may, however, mention one or two factors not hitherto emphasized. The first of these was the great overproduction of farm products, especially of wheat, and the consequent fall in prices. The rapid settlement of the public domain and the introduction of improved farm machinery resulted in the production of crops beyond the capacity of the domestic market to absorb, and whose export glutted the world-markets. Corn was so cheap that it was burned for fuel in many places, and wheat was left unharvested or fed to the stock. The agricultural overproduction and consequent depression adversely affected the railroads, banks, manufactures, and business in general.

A second feature making for maladjustment was the rapid exploitation of our mineral resources and the development of our great iron and steel industries. It was during this period that Jay Gould discovered that pig-iron production was the barometer of trade, but the fluctuations of the barometer unhappily introduced new elements of industrial instability.

Still a third factor was the currency disturbances, brought about by the efforts of Congress to force unneeded amounts of silver upon the country, and resulting in inflation, export of gold, and distrust.

The development before 1893 had been uneven and extreme, and the panic of that year had long been brewing. It was attended by banking and commercial failures, railroad bankruptcies, falling prices, reduced earnings, wage cuts, unemployment, strikes, distress, and unrest. A depression followed which continued until 1896, after which a revival of prosperity occurred which carried the nation to the highest standards of living yet enjoyed.

What shall we say of the crisis of 1929 and the subsequent depression? We are now in the trough and experiencing the pains of liquidation and readjustment but no one familiar with past panics can doubt that the cycle will again run its course and that we shall once more enjoy a greater prosperity. This is the lesson of history.

SOCIAL CONSEQUENCES OF BUSINESS DEPRESSIONS

Jane Addams

THERE are various traditions surrounding the man out of work, which inevitably influence our minds in periods of depression such as this. For many years in England the vagrant who entered a village was promptly clapped into the stocks and remained there sometimes for three days and three nights as a warning to all beholders, for if a man was idle he would be hungry, and if hungry, he would be likely to steal!

The element of discipline thus early recognized persists even among the very families of the unemployed. Simple women who do not read the papers nor see much of the outside world, keep closely to old patterns of conduct—wherein it is a man's business to work in order to support his family. An astonishing number of these women—ridden by fear lest their children starve—continually harass a disheartened husband who comes home from a futile search for work by the assertion that anyone can find work who really wants it. This attitude naturally

(12)

extends to the mother-in-law, who often takes home her married daughter with the little children "but will not feed *him*." To the overcrowding which ensues when one family moves into the already inadequate quarters occupied by another family, to the irritation which is so easily a by-product of anxiety, is added a profound sense of disapproval of the recreant husband and father out of work, which often results in permanent alienation.

In many ways in times of depression the stage is set for that most cruel and futile of all our undertakings—one human being punishing another in order to reform his character. This belief in punishment is reflected in the zeal with which we are sending out of the country every foreign-born man against whom some technical grounds for rejection can be found, "liable to become a public charge" being the one most often used. Compelled by economic conditions over which they have no control, many of them return with heavy hearts into more distress than that to which their unemployment had reduced them here. If it seems necessary because of economic reasons to do this harsh thing, surely it should be done because of necessity and not in the spirit of punishment of the immigrant because he is poor and jobless.

This disciplinary attitude toward a man out of work is largely founded upon two assumptions, both of them incorrect. One is that a man will not work unless driven by hunger, in spite of the well-

(13)

known physiological fact that hunger does not impel a man to work but so often saps his energies that in the end work may become impossible. The second is that the man does not wish to work, but deliberately chooses idleness. This latter assumption is based upon a mistaken idea of what leisure means to the poorest. The well-to-do man has plenty of pleasant ways to spend his leisure time. He can play golf, sit in a comfortable club with his friends, read in his own library, run the lawn mower over the grass. The poor man has only his crowded home, where a busy wife does not want him sitting around, or the street where he tramps weary hours looking for work, growing more humiliated with each rejection until leisure becomes a misery. Men have always paid a high price for lack of occupation! Perhaps, therefore, the first of the untoward social consequences of such a period of depression which we need to guard against, is the tendency to call a man a failure because he is out of work. It is always easy in America to judge a man by his success in business, to believe that he is receiving the rewards of virtue as well as the rewards of his ability and business acumen, which of course may or may not be true. It would be most unfortunate if we permitted this division into the virtuous successful and the reprehensible failures to become a permanent category.

Another consequence to be considered, and if possible avoided, is the lasting effect of such a period upon the vitality and ambition of thousands of our fellow-citizens. In 1919 Dr. Alice Hamilton and myself went with a group of English and American Quakers into Germany to report upon the effects on children of the prolonged underfeeding resulting from the war and the food blockade. We did not find that children had actually died of starvation although the death-rate was higher, but that the months of underfeeding, of never having had enough, had resulted in stunted growth, in rickets and tuberculosis, and in dulled minds and warped dispositions. It would be hard to tell how much of the difficulty in Europe since the war could have been composed without irritation and rancor if the young men who are now coming into power had had a more normal childhood.

We must remember that this is the second year of underfeeding for some families in the United States and the third year for others. What effect will it have on the coming generation? Already the tuberculosis rate is rising, the daily consumption of milk has been reduced in some cities by one-third, and the public school teachers in every city report a lowered vitality and loss of mental alertness on the part of the children from the poorer quarters.

We are in danger that the prolonged depletion of physical strength and mental vigor, affecting many men at the present moment, may menace the very sources of social progress. Nowhere is this more touchingly exhibited than among the young men and girls looking for work during the first year after they have left high school or college. They have been so elaborately prepared for the life which lay before them that it never occurred to them in all their getting ready that they would not be wanted when they at last arrived. The effect upon them of what the psychologists call "baulked disposition," the fact that a unique place in the world, which is so dear to the imaginations of the young, was not waiting for each one, wastes at the very beginning that precious enthusiasm which is so necessary in healing our social ills.

On the contrary, the consequences upon big industry have been encouraging in many ways. Early in the depression, the Proctor and Gamble Company, in Cincinnati, successfully stabilized employment throughout the year; the International Harvester and other great corporations have steadily lent money to their former employees upon the assumption of repayment when they should return to work; but perhaps the most encouraging of all is the plan recently announced by Gerard Swope, president of the General Electric Company, which advocates that each group of the great industries should regulate employment by the basic method of a careful estimate of the output required, as well as by providing unemployment insurance through the mutual efforts of all concerned. This plan also predicates governmental supervision. Its widespread discussion and favorable comment at least registers an approval of the fact that big industry is ready to hold itself responsible not only for its own un-employed, but also to avert the overproduction and lack of planning implicit in the situation itself.

Social consequences of such a period of depression will doubtless also be registered upon the practice of government. We have gradually found it possi-ble in the United States, in spite of our vaunted individualism, to provide state insurance of various sorts against the hazards of industry; almost every state makes provision of so-called "widows' pen-sions," that fatherless children may be properly cared for; seventeen states, including New York and California, have established old-age pensions and have found that to remove from the ranks of the unemployed thousands of elderly people in itself makes for stability. It is also true that it is cheaper to provide for an aged person with a pension than to care for him in the poorhouse. California saves thirteen dollars a month on each case thus provided for. Although the insurance funds are usually se-cured from the tax resources of the state at large, the administration of all these pension systems is naturally in the hands of local units of government. But in spite of this factor of local administration there seems to be a curious hesitancy in regard to unemployment insurance and a confusion in the public mind as to what it implies.

In any discussion of extending such provision to the unemployed, it is well to remember that ap-

(17)

proximately 70 per cent of the sources for relief during this entire period of depression have already come from public taxes. As few states and no counties or municipalities have power to levy taxes on incomes, these taxes have largely been paid by owners of real estate. In some cases this is manifestly unfair. We are told, for instance, that 6 per cent of the unemployed of the entire country are to be found in Detroit, and it would seem just that their maintenance should depend not upon the citizens of Detroit who own real estate there, but upon the stockholders living in various parts of the country, whose incomes have been derived from the industries centered in Detroit. In proportion as our great industries have become nation-wide in ownership, it would seem a normal process to support our unemployed by national taxation. It has in fact been suggested by a committee of able business men that it be done by an income tax of 1 per cent beginning with incomes of $1,000 and with surtaxes starting at lower brackets, but with a greater distinction than at present between earned and unearned incomes. This 1 per cent tax on all incomes should be retained by the government as an unemployment and old-age pension fund, with a commission to make it effective in co-operation with the states. These business men point out that the federal system of income tax is a going concern and would afford the most prompt method of securing relief in the present crisis. There may be a connection between this lack of income tax, or rather the theory of municipality tax versus national tax, and the fact that during sixty days last year in Detroit and its immediate vicinity, 50,000 small home owners were obliged to give up all equity in their property and to see the loss of their entire savings, because they could not earn the money either to meet the payments on their mortgages or to defray their taxes. Such a limitation of the taxation for the care of public charges to local units of government also works against the entire movement for the ownership of modest homes. A mine is closed, a factory about which a village centers is shut down, and the burden of relief falls upon the very men who are themselves in need of public help. The situation is less obvious in cities, but it exists there on a large scale.

Many immigrant families, who have been able to save money and finally to invest it in a house and lot, have lost both in this period of unemployment. After two or three years in a suburb, they return, defeated, to the neighborhood in which they first lived, obliged to lower their standard of living, to be received back into the households of relatives. In one month last spring thirty children who had lived in the suburbs came back to one school in the Hull-House district. Whether they miss the school more than their mothers miss the rows of vegetables in the garden or their fathers the dream of independent existence among prosperous Americans, it is hard to tell. The whole family are evidently mal-adjusted in the surroundings which they had so hopefully left, and it is doubtful whether they will ever make another start. Certainly they are frightened at the very notion of owning a house. Sometimes the equity in their property was small, but the sense of ownership was complete. It is the loss of such precious energy and ambition which may well become one of the most disastrous of the social consequences of the business depression.

Of course any such proposition that we meet the situation on a national scale, is at once countered by tales of disaster connected with the "dole" in England, which by no means settles the question. What is now called the "dole" in England is in fact a system of unemployment insurance started before the war, to which employers, workers, and the government contributed in almost equal amounts. With the breakdown of industry during the years following the war, the government, whether Conservative, Liberal, or Labor, has been obliged to bear the burden of paying the unemployment insurance. The English government would have been responsible in any case, because our Anglo-Saxon theory does not allow any man to starve. The national government in England has probably performed this service as effectively as any other unit of government could have done it. Certainly the almshouses could not have sheltered a modicum of the unemployed and their families, if the Poor-Law guardians had been held responsible and obliged to follow the beaten paths.

In the United States we cannot argue, in the face of the current $900,000,000 deficit in the federal treasury, that the absence of the "dole" insures us against budgetary troubles. While the resources of this country undoubtedly are much larger than those of Great Britain, it must be remembered that the threatened deficit which caused the crisis there is not more than one-quarter of our own; that the relief obtained by our unemployed from our improvised machinery is quite as injurious to self-respect as the benefits distributed at the British employment offices under definite provisions and public administration.

Two questions are before us in the United States: first, to determine how the funds necessary may be apportioned most fairly; and, second, how adequate provision may be made for our unfortunate fellow-citizens. We must not forget that a period of depression connotes vast human suffering and bewilderment, and that to avert disastrous social consequences is a primary obligation.

AMERICA AND THE BALANCE SHEET OF EUROPE

Harold G. Moulton

THE recent series of financial crises in European countries and the ensuing repercussions upon American finance and American foreign trade have brought a new realization of the economic unity of the world and of the degree to which American prosperity is linked with that of Europe. It is a curious fact, when one pauses to think about it, that this economic interdependency is apparent to the average observer only in periods of business reaction. During the recent boom era, for example, the view was very widespread that the United States had proved her economic independence of the rest of the world—that within our broad economic domain we had achieved economic self-sufficiency as well as discovered the secret of permanent prosperity. The relation between the expanding business of other countries during those years—an expansion made possible in large measure by American foreign loans—and American prosperity was so obscure as to be almost entirely ignored. But once the world-depression got under way and our export trade began to shrink, with accompanying disastrous effects upon the prices of our primary export products, it quickly became clear that our vaunted economic independence was without foundation.

The extent to which our exports to Europe have shrunk is, however, even now not fully appreciated. In the years 1926 to 1929 the value of our European shipments ranged around $2,300,000,000, annually. In 1930 it declined to $1,800,000,000; and during the first half of 1931 the value fell to a yearly rate of $1,200,000,000. Each succeeding month since March has shown further shrinkage, and the shipments to Europe are now smaller than in 1913—in actual volume as well as in terms of value.

It is reasonably clear from these figures that a fundamental requirement, if we are to have a return of real prosperity, is the stabilization of European financial conditions and the promotion of economic recovery there. I do not mean to imply that a business revival could not under any circumstances have its beginnings in the United States and then spread by gradual stages to the rest of the world. But I do mean that chaotic financial, economic, and social conditions such as exist in Europe at this juncture present a virtually insuperable barrier to economic recovery in this country. Constructive efforts toward world economic recuperation must therefore be focused upon Europe.

Before attempting to suggest ways in which an improvement in European economic conditions may be promoted, we must seek to appraise the nature of the economic difficulties with which central and western Europe have been confronted, not only in recent months but throughout the post-war era. It is fully appreciated by people everywhere that the World War resulted in an enormous destruction of wealth. But of greater importance—and this is not commonly recognized—were the economic and trade maladjustments which occurred. The normal economic balance between Europe and other countries, particularly the United States, was destroyed.

During the course of the World War the agriculture, the industry, and the finances of the European belligerents were thoroughly disorganized. In other countries, however, production and trade were expanded beyond all known bounds. The European shortage of commodities, coupled with an intensified demand, served like a protective tariff to stimulate new industries in nearly every non-belligerent country. This was true not only of the neutral nations of Europe, but the influence extended to North and South America, Australia, and the Orient as well. Moreover, agricultural production was enormously extended, particularly in Canada and the United States.

After the war was over the European belligerents naturally and of necessity sought to rehabilitate both their agriculture and their industry. The resuscitation of European agriculture which commenced shortly after the war inevitably lessened the demand for American and Canadian foodstuffs and precipitated an agricultural depression which has continued throughout the post-war era, even during periods of industrial prosperity.

The gradual industrial rehabilitation of Europe on the one hand lessens the demand for imported manufactured commodities, and on the other hand increases the European exports of manufactured goods. General economic recovery of Europe necessitates the recapture by the exporters of that continent of many formerly established markets, for the manufacturing nations of Europe depend upon exports of finished goods as a means of paying for imports of raw materials and foodstuffs.

It is readily apparent that such a process of recovery has not been welcome to those nations whose productive capacity has been so greatly expanded during the World War period. While the European nations have sought industrial and trade readjustments, other countries have endeavored to prevent such readjustment and to maintain the position which they had gained during the war. It is this fundamental conflict which accounts for the erection of new tariff barriers since the war and for the inability of the leading nations, either through their governments or international business organizations, to find a basis for harmonious international trade policies.

These fundamental trade difficulties accompanying the rising and falling of the economic tides produced by the World War have, moreover, been intensified as a result of the *financial* consequences of the war. In the first place, in the war and early post-war years the balance of international trade and financial relations was so profoundly altered that the private investors in these European nations lost a substantial part of their previously accumulated foreign holdings. With most nations the position shifted from that of creditor to that of debtor and in some instances, notably in the case of Germany, practically all foreign investments were lost. On the other hand, in the United States and Japan, Holland and the Scandinavian countries, and to a lesser extent elsewhere, the reverse occurred and these countries emerged as substantial creditors.

In addition to these great shifts in the balance of private international indebtedness, the war left a legacy of huge international governmental indebtedness. While the inter-allied indebtedness was incurred for value received, these war-time loans were not productive in character. Moreover, the reparation obligations imposed by the treaties of peace upon the Central Powers bore no relation whatever to economic enterprise. They were simply fines imposed for damages sustained.

The significance of these shifts in the relative financial position of the European belligerents is to be found in the long-run trade readjustments which the new relationships necessarily involve. A debtor nation must, if it is to meet its interest obligations, in the long run export more than it imports—this in order to obtain the foreign exchange with which to pay interest instalments abroad. Now the debtor countries, because of the maladjustments of the war period, to which reference has already been made, find it extremely difficult to earn the foreign exchange with which to meet their debts. The efforts of other countries to protect the new industries which developed during the war and to maintain their own exports inevitably handicap the exporting possibilities of the debtor countries.

The situation is particularly complex as it relates to the United States. This country's economic machine is geared to produce an enormous flow of goods for export—both agricultural commodities and industrial products. If our productive capacity is to be fully and efficiently employed, we need to maintain large exports. On the other hand, we have been endeavoring to keep imports at a minimum, our tariff being designed to protect American industry, and to a less extent agriculture, from foreign competition. Thus, we strive to maintain a large export surplus when the economic requirements of reparation and war-debt payments necessitate an import surplus.

During recent years we have temporarily avoided the dilemma of collecting debts, without receiving an excess of imports, by means of new loans to Europe. That is to say, instead of getting out of debt, Europe—speaking generally—has been going even further into debt. To illustrate by reference to Germany—the nation which is supposed to provide the wealth for the liquidation of all the war debts—that country has since the inauguration of the Dawes Plan in 1924 borrowed about two dollars for every dollar paid on reparation account. It has been the thought—or rather the hope—that this process might be continued indefinitely, thereby avoiding at least until some remote future day the trade readjustments that are required if the reparation obligation is finally to be collected.

These huge loans, amounting between 1924 and 1930 to approximately $4,000,000,000, moreover obscured the basic economic problems of Germany. For the time being the loans promoted buoyant economic activity and prevented any possible exchange crisis. It was thus possible for superficial observers to believe that Germany had completely recovered from the war, and also that it had been demonstrated that both the reparation and inter-allied debt obligations could be met according to schedule without in anywise adversely affecting our trade.

But it was only a few months after new credits ceased to be extended that Germany's finances broke down and the country was threatened with a repetition of the tragic conditions of 1923. Emphasis is placed upon the German situation because it is at the heart of the whole problem of the war debts, the inter-allied debt payments having been closely articulated with reparation receipts.

With the prompt and courageous policy announced by this government last June in favor of a complete moratorium on reparation and inter-allied debt payments for the period of a year, this vexatious problem entered upon a new phase. As a result of the economic events of the past year, we are now in a position to consider more clearly than ever before the economics of this problem. The fundamental question is whether our own prosperity and that of the world as a whole will best be promoted by eliminating so far as possible those factors which produce unbalanced trade relations and by enlarging European purchasing power. It needs to be clearly borne in mind in this connection that every dollar which the European nations turn over to us in liquidation of war-time obligations means a dollar that cannot be used by them to purchase American exports. Reduced purchases of our products means reduced prices of export commodities, and these in turn mean decreased earnings and decreased tax-paying capacity on the part of American agriculture and American industry. While our export trade accounts for a relatively small percentage of our total trade, its curtailment leads to severe depression of basically important industries, and this in turn has its repercussions upon the entire business structure. The potential tax revenues that might be collected from profitable American business greatly outweigh the gains to the Treasury from the collection of war debts.

Thoroughgoing economic recovery in the United States is not to be expected until financial stability can be established in Europe and until the financial and trade maladjustments which resulted from the World War are in substantial measure eliminated. Some of the maladjustments produced by the war cannot be readily overcome. But the artificial ones resulting from the war debts may be eliminated—difficult though the political aspects of the problem still are. In conclusion, I would emphasize again the basic fact that a state of balanced trade between Europe and America is a prime essential for the prosperity of both continents.

INTERNATIONAL ECONOMIC
INTERDEPENDENCE

Edwin F. Gay

A FRIEND, several months ago, wrote me that he had recently examined a business situation which brought home to him concretely the meaning of international economic interdependence. He found that the financial position of a concern in the eastern part of the United States was endangered because it could not collect a considerable debt from a company on the Pacific Coast. The California company explained that its default was due to the fact that it could not obtain payments from a large export firm doing business in the Malay States. On further inquiry it was discovered that credit was also frozen in that distant region because the Malayan tin miners found themselves, in the midst of world-wide business depression, unable to compete with the superior efficiency of the tin mines in Bolivia.

Nearly every business man, if he could follow the movement of his wares and credits both before and after they enter his control, would find that he is intimately bound in the vast network of exchanges over the globe. Ordinarily the great interlocking mechanism of world-trade works swiftly and silently. Until the recent shock of a world-depression most of us were unaware of its operation. Indeed, we have often heard that our country, with its enormous resources and its continental market, is substantially self-sufficient. Only a few days ago, a prominent senator, in making this point, called attention to the fact that our export trade amounts to only about 10 per cent of the total national production. The witness before his committee answered by saying that "it's the last 10 per cent that makes business profitable or unprofitable."

The answer did not go far enough. It is true that with the growth of plant capacity in our large-scale industrial units this 10 per cent foreign outlet has become increasingly important. But much more important than the comparatively small flow of export merchandise is the influence of foreign trade on our whole price and credit structure. Almost all our wholesale prices are fundamentally determined by the conditions of supply and demand in the world-market. This influences not only the prices of the great export staples, like cotton and wheat, copper and petroleum, and the manufactured goods, like automobiles and machinery, which on a large scale enter into direct international competition for the demand of the world, but it extends to the wide range of commodities of which we export only a small fraction of our production, and even to those which we export not at all.

Milk, for instance, is the typical "domestic" product, too perishable for exportation, but milk in the form of butter, cheese, and condensed milk yearly contributes two and a half billion pounds to the volume of the world's export trade, and foreign prices on dairy products influence the local prices of fluid milk in all parts of the United States. This case also illustrates the marked widening of the field of foreign trade characteristic of recent decades. With the steady advance in preservative processes— canning, drying, condensing, refrigerating—and with the corresponding increase in the facilities of transportation by land and sea, practically the whole group of "perishables" has been transferred from the category of local commodities to that largely subject to the prices of the international market.

Raw materials, for the most part highly sensitive to the price movements of the world, form a major element in the cost of all manufactured goods. The wholesale prices of these products are in turn basic for retail prices in the home market. There are, of course, lags and differentials, due, as between countries, to tariffs and market frictions, as well as the costs of transportation, but, despite all impediments, the general price-level indices which the statisticians have set up for a number of countries show a remarkable parallelism.

It would be interesting, if we had time, to show how prices react on one another, how they are diffused geographically, how they compete as between wares and as between industries for the consumer's dollar, how a multitude of alert traders, flashing price quotations, offers, and bids by telegraph, cable, and radio, tie the whole system of prices together. The entire fabric of commodity prices, woven continuously, stretches over the world, and every invention, whether of new synthetic substitutes or of communications, binds the continents closer together. Even if high tariffs or hostile patent laws interpose obstacles, capital and management migrate freely and thus reinforce international economic interdependence.

There exists in the system of prices a group which is marked by considerable but varying rigidities. The prices of labor and services, of buildings and real estate, of the products of public utilities, such as transportation, power, light, and water, seem at first sight to be little responsive to international influences. But even these are not wholly immune, for if not their rates at any rate their earnings fluctuate more or less laggingly with the ebb and flow of business activity, and these cyclical variations tend increasingly to correspond with those in other countries of high economic development.

What has been said concerning the international interdependence of prices is also true of credit and of interest, which is the price of credit. The modern growth of transportation and communication has brought a steadily extending area of the world under the sway of a credit economy. Practically all wholesale trade, the world over, is on credit, and in the leading countries retail trade, especially in the form of installment buying, has experienced a great extension of credit to consumers. Even though the actual flow of credit, by means of its numerous instruments, from one country to another, is small compared with the volume of the domestic flow, nevertheless the price of credit and its domestic volume has become highly sensitive to foreign influence. The stresses and strains, like those in the whole price system, are variously distributed and unevenly transmitted, but they ultimately affect all parts of the system, and, if the shock to credit be severe, like the one we have recently witnessed, it may spread rapidly through the family of nations and involve not only multitudes of men but even governments. The stream of credit in normal times irrigates and fertilizes wide tracts, national and international, in the roundabout processes of commerce and industry. But when it contracts, perhaps because it has been wastefully used, the far-reaching enterprises which link country to country must suffer.

International trade in goods and credit is nothing new. It has gone on for centuries. But the scale to which it has developed, the extent to which countries in their economic life have become interlocked, is something new. It is a difference of degree which has the proportions of a difference in kind. The Industrial Revolution, as during the nineteenth century it unfolded and widened, ultimately created in many countries huge organizations and aggregations of enterprises, operating in great markets and implemented by world-wide agencies of transport and finance. It was a Victorian boast that this process had made the world smaller, but before the World War it had not created a corresponding enlargement of the sense of national responsibilities. A fundamental transformation in the world economic situation had already taken place; no country could any longer be a hermit kingdom; no country was any longer self-sufficing. All were inescapably joined by bonds of economic interest, by a web of contract prices and credits, woven not by statesmen or cosmopolitan visionaries or even mainly by international financiers, but by the ceaseless efforts of tens of thousands of business men and by the migrations and rising standards of living of millions of working men and women.

The world was becoming an economic unit, but we were not aware of it. We had been told that the United States was a world-power, but we did not realize what that entailed. For a century we had turned our backs upon Europe in order to subjugate a continent; we had become populous and wealthy. But when the World War broke out in Europe, our minds harked back to that former great European war whose close we had witnessed a century before when we were a weak neutral power at the beginning of our national life. It was understandable, therefore, that from 1914 to 1917 we were, as a people, reluctant to enter a war which we thought concerned European interests alone. But we found that it concerned the whole world and our own future as a vital world-force. The war revealed the community of nations, and the need for common protective action. And now the deep business depression encompassing the world, with its broken prices and successive shocks to credit, has been a second lesson in world-consciousness.

That there exists a community of interests among the people of the world, that this community has been steadily growing during the past century and is destined to develop stronger agencies of common action, is not merely a fanciful version of history. It rests solidly upon the facts of our economic and social experience, painfully suffered at the time of the war and at this present time of the war's economic aftermath. But the existence of a nationalism enhanced in vigor is equally a fact of history and of present observation. The war intensified nationalism, with us as with other nations. For a decade we have clung to the old illusion of self-sufficiency, keeping ourselves as aloof as possible from the European entanglements we once—and for good reason then—had been taught to dread. Abroad the war gave birth to new national states; it left the nations keen-

ly ambitious to rebuild their own shattered structure. Although they have been also anxious to repair
the rough gaps torn in the old fabric of economic relationships, they one and all have remained appre-
hensive of each other. Every nation feels intensely
the need of security for itself. How can the realization be brought to self-centered nations that the
safety of each lies in the common security of all?

Despite all its selfish, strife-breeding jealousies, nationalism is a force to be respected. It has been and
remains the strongest agency we possess for molding
into effective cohesion great social groups. No surrender of nationalism, but a greater co-operation between nations, is now required.

Widespread recognition of the need for international co-operation and a national willingness to
take the responsibility of definite steps toward co-
operative action are fundamental to any such con-
crete measures as a modification of tariff barriers, of
reparations and debt agreements, or of the organization of monetary standards and of international
credits. We cannot fail to realize that our own economic and social problems are to an ever growing
degree not merely local and national in character.
The recovery from unemployment and from "frozen
credits" in the United States is largely dependent on
the recovery of the political and economic confidence of our neighbors abroad. This is a strong
country, and in any case, even unaided and unaiding,
we shall somehow recover. But the recovery will be

speedier and sounder and for the future we shall incur less danger of another equally deep and disastrous depression if we are ready to support the present or any subsequent administration in entering into close and continuous international co-operation. Perhaps, as a nation, we might be happier—though I doubt it—could we put the clock back to the relatively greater self-sufficiency of fifty or a hundred years ago. But the laws of growth are inexorable. As the world grows smaller, we must grow larger minded.

That is the meaning today of international economic interdependence.

EFFECTS OF DEPRESSIONS ON EMPLOY-
MENT AND WAGES

William M. Leiserson

THE effects of depressions on employment and wages are, of course, known to all of you in a general way. You know that when a depression comes employment is reduced. People are discharged or laid off. Those who remain at work have their earnings reduced by working short time. Wage rates are cut, and those of the unemployed who get new jobs must take them at lower pay. One does not need to be an economist to know that these are the effects of industrial depressions.

But though we all know these obvious effects, what are the remedies that we advise and adopt to overcome them? We advise and we practice economy. Business men lay off more people, work more short time, reduce wages more. And we tell the government to do the same; to spend less, to cut salaries, to lay off employees. In other words, we believe the best way to overcome the problems of reduced employment and wages is to go on reducing employment and wages some more. For people who are suffering because they have lost wages and income we prescribe more of the same medicine.

Can you imagine any greater miracle than that employment and wages should be restored by reducing employment and wages more and more? If recovery actually comes by this method we shall witness a miracle the equal of which is hardly to be found in the holy books of any nation. But whether recovery results from this policy, or does not, our present belief that more unemployment and more losses in wages is a cure for unemployment and wage losses would seem to mark the limit of faith in miracles. However, as G. K. Chesterton has recently pointed out, the depression itself is a miraculous phenomenon surpassing any of those recounted in biblical narratives. No miracle in the Bible asks us to believe that people were ever faced with starvation because they had too many loaves and fishes. If we were not living through the present depression, it certainly would be unbelievable that hundreds of thousands of people should be without food because too much wheat and corn and milk had been produced.

Why do we believe in, and why do we perform such miracles? There are many reasons, no doubt. But one of the most important is our naïve faith that something to which we have given the high-sounding name, "Natural Economic Law," knows better than human beings do what is best for mankind. A famous forecasting and statistical organization, much patronized by business men, recently wrote to its subscribers: "The time-tested law of supply and demand must be allowed a free hand;—monkeying with fundamentals will not hasten business recovery." Would any sensible person nowadays say that the time-tested law of gravitation must be allowed a free hand—to sink ships, to drop bridges, or to topple skyscrapers? So long as we stand in helpless, superstitious fear of economic laws, which are natural in only an academic sense, we shall believe in and be witnesses to economic miracles.

When we brush aside such superstitious fears and examine the facts of employment and wages in a sensible manner, we discover that they are governed by the laws of business and not by the laws of nature. And business, far from being natural, is about as artificial a contrivance as man has ever created to aid him in getting a living. Because business is interested in labor costs per unit of product, rather than in incomes for wage-earners and their families, our information about employment and earnings is tabulated and published after the manner of commodity statistics. Employment is reported by the day, week, or month. Wages are given by the piece, or per hour, per day, and per week. For buyers and sellers, these unit measures, comparable to the prices of commodities, are of great value. It is by watching such statistics that business men know when and how to cut wages and to reduce employment. But for a nation interested in work for its adult population, and in steady incomes the year around for all its people, such market measures are very misleading, as will presently appear.

In 1929, our last prosperous year, the total earnings of those of our people who work for wages and salaries amounted to something like 55 billion dollars. In 1930, the first year of the depression, and before its effects had attained their full force, these wages and salary payments were reduced approximately 10 billion dollars. During the first nine months of the present year, pay-rolls have been about 30 per cent lower than in 1929, and the multiplication of wage-cutting, following the example of the steel industry, as well as the seasonal decline in employment that usually comes during the winter months, will probably bring earnings for the year down close to 40 per cent below 1929. This means that wage and salary payments will be between 18 and 20 billion dollars less this year than in 1929.

In terms of employment, the effect of these losses is the same as if six million five hundred thousand workers were totally unemployed in 1930, with no earnings whatsoever. In the present year, the effect is equivalent to 13 million unemployed for the whole year. Actually, however, the losses are not concentrated on one group of wholly unemployed people. They are widely distributed by part-time work, rotation in employment, and cuts in rates of pay, as well as by laying off and discharging employees. The result is that the reduction in the numbers on the pay-rolls is not as great as the reduction in wages and earnings.

Ten years ago we had a similar depression. It did not last as long as the present one, but the effects were pretty much the same. The total wages paid was lower by more than six billion dollars in 1921 than in 1920; a reduction of 21 per cent, while employment dropped 16 per cent. For the major industrial depressions prior to 1921 we have but few reliable statistics on which to base estimates. We know, however, that wages paid in manufacturing, transportation, and mining in 1908 were about 16 per cent below 1907, and in 1894 they were 24 per cent below 1892.

Now if we are to do anything to prevent or to reduce these losses and to safeguard the means of livelihood for the vast majority of the families of the nation, we must know whether the reductions in incomes are inevitable decrees of economic law, with which we must not "monkey," as the business experts put it, or whether our economic arrangements can be so changed and controlled as to eliminate the poverty and suffering that the depressions bring upon us. Fortunately, the development of business management during the last twenty-five or thirty years offers us a clue to the answer to this question.

Economists often say that business executives, captains of industry, or in the terminology of economics, the entrepreneurs, are the pay-masters of the nation. They pay out not only wages and salaries to employees, but also interest to investors, dividends to stockholders, rent to landlords. If we examine what happens in times of depression to these different kinds of income, it becomes plain that our pay-masters have somehow managed to guard those who invest capital in industry against losses of income such as the workers suffer.

In 1930, for example, while the workers' earnings were reduced by 10 billion dollars, the payments made by business corporations in interest on bonds and dividends on stock actually increased by 900 million dollars. Interest payments alone were 270 million dollars greater in the first year of depression than in the prosperous year 1929. Dividends paid on stock in 1930 were more than 600 million dollars above those paid the preceding year. We are now in the second year of the depression, and while our pay-masters have found it necessary to reduce wage payments by about one-third, they have managed to increase their interest payments for the first eight months of the year 100 million dollars over the amount paid in the corresponding months of last year, and 300 million dollars over the same months in 1929. Dividend payments this year have declined to some extent. Up to and including August, total dividends paid were about 200 million dollars less than for the same period in 1930; but they were still 600 million dollars more than the dividends paid at the height of prosperity in 1929.

Turning to the depression of 1921 we find that much the same thing happened. While wages were reduced 21 per cent, interest payments increased in the depression by 71 million dollars over the preceding prosperous year. Dividend payments were maintained in 1921 to within 5 per cent of the amount distributed in 1920. And as final evidence of what our business executives have done to stabilize prosperity incomes, we have the fact that in every single year from 1909 to date, interest payments increased over the preceding year, regardless of prosperity or depression, and regardless also of the changes in value of the dollar.

In the depressions of the nineteenth century business proprietors, bondholders, stockholders, and wage-workers all suffered alike; there was a universal lowering of standards of living. In the twentieth century, however, business managers have learned how to stabilize interest and dividends; and, apparently, the more responsibility they have come to feel for maintaining the incomes of investors, the more they find themselves under the necessity of reducing the wages of their employees. Why should natural economic law require that wages be reduced drastically in times of depression, while incomes in the form of interest and dividends must be increased, or maintained as closely as possible to the levels of the years of prosperity? Bear in mind that dividends are profits and the system of private enterprise assumes the profit-maker will bear the inevitable risks of business. The wage-earner is supposed to take no business risks.

It is in this connection that the misleading nature of our wage statistics becomes most evident. In order to save money on the wages bill so that interest and dividends may be paid, many employers compare wage rates with commodity prices and tell us that wages must be adjusted to the reductions in prices. But wages in terms of the earnings of working people are already 35 per cent below 1929, whereas cost of living has declined less than 15 per cent. Moreover, efficiency and productiveness of workers employed have measurably increased during the last two years.

To a worker whose earnings have been cut in half by unemployment and part-time work it must seem like a grim joke to get an additional wage reduction because living costs have declined 10 or 15 per cent. The result of wage-cutting in past depressions was always to push wages down lower than living costs declined; in other words, to reduce standards of living. Real wages, or the purchasing power of money wages, fell 16 per cent in 1921, and 12 per cent in each of the depressions of 1908 and 1894. This may have been necessary when interest and dividends were cut as drastically as wages. But, today, it is important to note, if wage-earners' incomes are cut it is done in order that the incomes of bondholders and stockholders may be paid.

I conclude, therefore, that the effects of depres-

sions on employment and wages are not brought
about by any unseen force or natural law, but by
human beings in the form of employers and directors
of corporations, who wish to accomplish certain,
definite, human purposes. They choose to maintain
the incomes of those who invest money in industry
because they think that the maintenance of the
property investment is more important than the
maintenance of the labor investment. When they
come to feel that incomes for wage-earners and
maintenance for the families dependent on them are
as important as interest and dividend payments,
they will stabilize wages too.

Already some of our more foresighted business
leaders have set up reserves for the maintenance of
wages, similar to the reserves provided for the
maintenance of property and the incomes of investors. They do not consider that payments made
to workers, who are unemployed through no fault
of their own, are doles any more than payments to
investors are doles when their machinery and factories are not working or are only partially employed. But most of the owners and directors of our
industries will continue to decry the viciousness of
doles and to believe in the beneficence of natural
economic law for many years to come. We can hardly wait until they learn how to abolish unemployment.

Those who heard Professor Bogart open this series
of radio talks with a description of the depressions

of the last century must have been impressed by the fact that free, enterprising business, with freedom to consumers to choose what they will buy, cannot be maintained without a serious depression every ten or twenty years. Already we have had two such depressions in the present century; and one must be blind indeed to the conditions of modern economic life to believe that this is the last of the depressions. It is well to talk about making work steady, but who believes that efforts in this direction will provide a job in the future for every family breadwinner that is able and willing to work? We will emerge from this depression, of course; but just as surely as prosperity is bound to return, so also is depression, unemployment, and loss of livelihood for millions of wage-earners bound to return.

It is necessary, therefore, that the citizens and tax-payers of the country serve notice on American industry and its managers that we do not propose in future depressions to subsidize them by supporting their employees from private and public charity funds. We must make it the duty of all employers of labor to carry insurance against the disasters that recurring depressions bring to their working forces. When employers of labor can no longer depend on the community to maintain their workers in times of depression, they will find a way of providing unemployment reserve and insurance funds to put wage payments on at least as stable a basis as they have put interest and dividends.

(49)

BUSINESS DEPRESSIONS AND BUSINESS PROFITS

William F. Gephart

PERIODS of business depression, such as the present, have been occurring, on the average, from two to three times in each generation. In broad outline each of these periods has shown a marked similarity to those that have preceded it. Each depression has been characterized by widespread unemployment, numerous business failures, curtailed profits in all lines of business, and by a general undermining of public confidence in the existing economic order. Since we are to discuss profits and depressions it is well to understand: first, the nature and character of profit and the rôle it plays in our economic and social organization; and second, the characteristics of depressions, as well as something of their causes, duration, and frequency.

Our prevailing industrial organization is characterized by private property, free contract, competition, and profit-seeking. Profit may be defined as that amount left after the elementary costs of production are met—namely, wages, rent, and interest.

It is a residual claimant. As an incentive to economic effort, profit is unquestionably of primary importance. Some of the economic results of the effort to obtain profits are inventions, discoveries, and the placing on the market of new products, or cheaper or better products, because it is only as an individual producer does this that he is able to obtain the market from a competitor, or by increased consumption of the product secure a profit.

There are at the present time many critics of the existing industrial organization and some who seem to have lost all faith in it. This state of mind arises from a lack of knowledge of the history of social and industrial progress. If there is any one development during the past one thousand years more striking than another, it is the increasing power and control which the masses of people have over their political, social, and industrial organizations. Political, as well as industrial, enfranchisement has been the most marked development of the past several centuries. In the ten thousands of years that man has existed, he has experimented with various kinds of political, social, and industrial institutions. China, for example, several thousand years ago tried Socialism, but found it lacking.

Man has progressed most rapidly in his culture and arts when he has enjoyed a large degree of personal freedom, and when free scope has been given to his individual enterprise and initiative, and when as a result of this larger freedom he has been able to enjoy the fruits of his personal efforts, whether this result has expressed itself in profits or other monetary gains or, as more often has been the case, in the pleasure he derived in seeing the fruits of his own individual enterprise.

In ancient times the king, the emperor, the despot prescribed the rules for the individual in his industrial, social, and political activities. At present, there seem to be those who think a dictator or a soviet régime with a few in control can best direct man's activities. The despot of ancient times and the dictator of the present, whether an individual or a soviet régime, are essentially no different. In either case it is primarily the direction of the life of the many by the few, and no individual or small group of individuals is wise enough to determine the best systems of social and industrial organization which will bring the greatest happiness. Permanent progress must be based not upon what man ought to want, but upon what he thinks he wants. Human progress comes about from a happy compromise between what the wisest think man should have and what in fact man actually wants. Our present industrial organization with its individual competition, free contract, and private property is not a result of chance, nor has it been superimposed on man. It is a historical development which has resulted from experimentation with many different kinds of organization. It is, therefore, contrary to the social evolution of the past to assume that man will revert to centralized control by one or a few. The hard-earned victory that man has gained from his thousands of years of sacrifice to give free scope to his individual freedom of action in political, social, and industrial activities will not be surrendered for the glittering and false hopes of a utopian society wherein the individual has no personal responsibilities and duties but only rights and privileges. Social progress is the resultant of the sum total of individual accomplishments, and there is no mysterious, magical way by which man can progress except by his individual efforts.

There is mingled good and evil in every man and in every one of his institutions, but painfully and slowly social progress is achieved and man satisfies his wants with decreasing sacrifice and pain. He devises under a régime of individual liberty new agencies and new institutions to serve his needs. They work now well, now badly. He uses them. He abuses them, but they are his own agencies and are not enforced upon him. He learns to read and write, but he writes and reads much that should never be written or read. He gains wealth from his profitable activities and misuses it. It may not profit him to gain the whole world and lose his own soul, but others profit by his failures. He has painfully acquired a status as an individual, as one who has the right and the power to determine his institutions.

We want and have earned the privilege of making mistakes, blunders, and even failures in order that we may enjoy the pleasure and the success of the results of our efforts. Therefore, let those who indict the present organized competitive society for its profit-seeking, for its misuse of personal wealth, for its exploitation of man, and the waste of natural resources recall the teachings of history. Let them review the acts of the despots and the centralized control of an earlier period under which the people were enslaved and exploited and when war was but an amusement for the rulers. Let them evaluate in the terms of history the present efforts of dictators to direct minutely the lives of millions of people and then let them compare the progress of man and the increase in human happiness and general well-being under the earlier period of centralized control and the latter period of individual freedom.

Under a privately organized society each seeks to place on the market the largest possible volume of goods under the favorable conditions of increasing price levels, and this periodically leads to a maladjustment between the supply of and the effective demand for goods.

Notwithstanding that these recurring periods of maladjustment between production and consumption result, there is no definitely established periodicity for these cycles of depression. They follow no established law with respect to their intervals or their intensity. This must necessarily be true when one considers the multiplicity of factors which determine industrial prosperity or depression.

There may be, for example, a period of great inventions, scientific discoveries, and rapid technological progress which fundamentally affects industrial activity. There may be, on the other hand, disastrous conditions of weather and other natural phenomena over which man has no control. Or again, there may be periods of war and political and social unrest. Each of these does and will continue to affect and give direction to periods of prosperity and depression. It is, therefore, well within reason to state that these maladjustments will occur under our system of privately organized industrial society and there is equally no reason to believe that any other system of industrial organization would prevent them or would not have within it evils equally great.

Nevertheless, much can be done to bring about a better co-ordination of production and consumption and improve the organization of the credit machinery not only national but international. This relief is to be found primarily in permitting a greater degree of co-operation, not only among the individual business units in a particular industry or nation, but also in world-wide co-operation. The old maxim that competition is the life of trade is no longer true. Today it is co-ordination and co-operation and not competition which gives not only continued life to trade, but also a healthful condition of trade over the intervening years.

Notwithstanding the fact that business profits

during periods of business depression are not only severely reduced, and often completely eliminated, the fact remains that this is but a transitory phenomenon. From the available material covering the past century, together with considerable detail for the past one-third of a century, there is every evidence that periods of business depression have only a retarding influence on the underlying trend of corporate profits. No major depression of the past century has resulted in reversing, for more than a very short period, the generally upward trend of industrial earnings.

The same thing is true with respect to wages; notwithstanding the fact that money wages usually show some decline during periods of depression, none of the past depressions has resulted in any ultimate decrease in either money or real wages for the longer term period.

The relation between profits and price level is one of great importance, both in its direct and indirect influences. On the average, during periods of increasing prices, profits are likely to be higher than the regular factors determining net earnings would of themselves produce. This is true principally because the business man secures not only his normal profit on manufacturing or merchandising, but, in addition, the gains resulting from a general price increase of both his raw and finished products. He may also benefit through the relative reduction in such fixed charges as interest on borrowed capital and from the benefits of owning plant and equipment costing less than its reproduction value new. Profits, therefore, at such times are likely to be higher and increase at even a greater percentage than either the volume of goods sold or the percentage increase in the price level. On the converse, during periods of decline in the level of commodity prices, earnings are likely to be proportionately restricted for the same reasons. Apparently, during periods of relative price stability, the opportunity for sound profits is greatest.

Business profits then, during depressions, are adversely affected, first, by smaller volumes of output, second, by lower price per unit of product, and third, by inventory losses resulting from raw material price declines. In order to study the effects of these three factors upon industrial earnings, during the major depressions of the present century, we have compiled statistics covering the net available for dividends of a group of corporations making up a selected cross-section of American industry. For the period from 1900 to 1914, twenty large corporations were used and from 1915 to date twenty-five were included in this study. This group consists of the leading business concerns in each of the major industries. In 1929, this group of corporations reported a total net income of over one billion dollars. All corporations reporting to the Treasury Department reported a net income in that year of about six billion, five hundred million dollars. Thus it will be seen that this group represents corporations reporting almost one-sixth of the total corporate income of the country and, as a consequence, should constitute a fairly good sample of the earnings experience of the larger and better-known industries of the country. This group, although representative of industry generally, is not necessarily a criterion of individual experience. The figures compiled by the Treasury Department, covering the period from 1916 to 1930, show that a large number of corporations report deficits every year regardless of the general state of trade. They reveal, for example, that only 66 per cent of all corporations in 1917 reported a net income and that in 1921 only 48 per cent reported a net income. Furthermore, from 1920 to 1929, a period generally regarded as one of prosperity, the average annual deficit of corporations reporting to the Treasury Department has been in excess of two billion dollars each year. Thus, it is at once clear that even during prosperous times a great many business concerns not only earn no net income but suffer substantial deficits.

In the period from 1901 to 1914, the earnings, of all corporations used in this study, show an average annual increase of about 1.25 per cent. For the period from 1915 to 1920, the average annual increase amounts to about 6.2 per cent. Therefore, notwithstanding the fact that in the pre-war period from 1900 to 1914, business suffered from three depressions, the underlying trend of corporate earnings was upward. While earnings showed a substantial decline during the year 1904, most of the loss was recovered in 1905 and a new high level reached in both 1906 and 1907. Following the depression, which began in 1907, corporate earnings showed a sizable recession for 1908 but within two years again re-established a new high level. In the depression of 1914, corporate profits again recorded a sizable recession but within two years had gone into new high ground. Following 1921, corporate profits re-established their previous prosperity levels within two years and established new high records in each of the next succeeding five years. The evidence of this study indicates that depressions have but a temporary influence on the underlying trend of corporate profits. While the decline in profits may be sharper than its succeeding rise, it seldom takes more than a few years for industrial earnings to recover not only all that is lost during a depression but they have invariably gone into new high ground within a few years.

If we examine the pre-war period from 1900 in somewhat greater detail, we find that during the depression of 1907–08 business volume, as measured by the index of business activity, declined about 25 per cent; commodity prices decreased almost $12\frac{1}{2}$ per cent; and business profits dropped about 26 per cent. In other words, the shrinkage in profits was something more than the drop in prices, but approximated the decline in volume. During the recession of

1913–14, business volume receded about 21 per cent; commodity prices decreased almost 10 per cent; and earnings over 26 per cent. In this period it will be noted that earnings were more severely affected than either prices or volume. In 1920–21 business volume decreased about 34 per cent and prices dropped over 49 per cent while earnings dropped almost 64 per cent. In this instance earnings followed the pattern of the preceding recession, declining to a greater extent than either prices or volume. For the present depression, up to July, 1931, volume showed a decline of about 40 per cent and prices of over 32 per cent. While the final figures for corporate earnings for 1931 are not yet available, we know that corporate earnings declined over 25 per cent during 1930, and various estimates place the decline in 1931 at from 35 to 50 per cent from the levels of 1929, thus again indicating that the decline in profits will be larger than either that of volume or prices.

The behavior of business profits in different lines of industry during and immediately following depressions, is by no means uniform. A more detailed analysis of the earnings of selected industries is available in the printed paper covering this address. This includes such industries as steel, non-ferrous metals, building, electrical equipment, rubber, tobacco, and textiles to show how profits are affected in periods of depression and prosperity.

It would, therefore, seem fairly clear from an

analysis of corporation profits during the past thirty years that:

a) as might be inferred, corporation net profits generally are adversely affected by periods of depression, but that

b) fluctuations in earnings for different industries vary greatly. The newer and developing industries, such as electrical and chemical, and the public utilities, show, on the whole, a higher degree of stability and growth than most other lines;

c) the profits in the older industries, such as woolens, cotton, leather, and rubber, whose raw materials are subjected to international competition, are likely to be less stable than many other industries;

d) those industries depending more largely for profits on skilful business and marketing organizations, such as the food distributing industries, are not likely to be so adversely affected by periods of depression. This is largely true because the efficiency in marketing or distributing goods is far behind that of producing them and there exists much opportunity in the future for profitable enterprise in this field of economic activity;

e) on the whole, the evidence of this study indicates that periods of depression result in severe decline or total elimination of corporate profits for short periods only;

f) as a result of the elimination of unsound and extravagant business policies they invariably lay the foundation for a substantial recovery in corporate earnings power within a relatively short period and ultimately result in the attainment of new high levels for business profits.

AGRICULTURE IN RELATION TO
ECONOMIC PROSPERITY

Edwin G. Nourse

SOME people will tell you that the present economic depression hit agriculture first and spread, like the measles, from farmers to city dwellers. Then they will add that you can't expect general business conditions to become satisfactory again until the farmer is prosperous and good times spread from him to other lines of business. People who see things in this light are likely to propose desperate remedies, these remedies to be applied directly to farm prices. All around us they are urging bounties on exports and buying by stabilization corporations, or insisting that acreage be reduced or crops destroyed until sheer scarcity shall force farm prices up. These devices, they say, will restore rural prosperity and in due time cause the whole economic system to revive.

This line of reasoning is unduly influenced by analogies from the past, particularly the severe depressions of 1873–78 and 1893–96. In those days, while we were still preponderantly an agricultural

(63)

country, selling farm exports to the industrial markets of Europe, agricultural distress was almost synonymous with national depression. On the other hand, the coincidence of a big crop at home and a short crop abroad, as in 1878 and 1879 and again in 1897 and 1898, appeared as the strong reviving factor causing business conditions in the United States to overcome depression and inaugurate a period of prosperity.

But if we attempt to apply such a theory of business cycles to conditions as we find them today, we encounter difficulties. Agriculture has suffered depression continuously, though in varying degrees of intensity, since 1920, while industry enjoyed an early recovery from the post-war decline and had several years of rather exceptional prosperity before the crash of 1929. Forces operating directly upon agriculture caused a prolonged depression in this particular industry which, however, has run its course largely independent of the cycle of general business. Special factors caused an uncontrollable expansion of farm production at the very time when conditions of demand in the world-market were such as to point the need of curtailment or at least effective control of output. This, of course, held farm prices down even when other commodities recovered.

Meanwhile our farmers kept doggedly at the task of working out their own adjustment to this difficult situation. They have changed their methods of farming, abandoned unsuitable areas, and brought in superior new ones. They have shifted from horses to tractors, developed new combinations of crops and new methods for producing and marketing them. They have to a considerable extent reorganized their business. They have maintained and even expanded output while reducing unit costs of production. We have it on the authority of the United States Department of Agriculture that American farmers increased efficiency 15 per cent in the post-war decade. Volume of production in fruits and vegetables, meat and dairy products, and cotton had increased by 1929 all the way from 10 to 40 per cent from the level at which they stood at the end of the war. Grains were the only important group that fell off—about 12 per cent. And while this growth in output was taking place some half-million farmers (with their families) were leaving the farm to join the ranks of urban labor.

Anyone who knows anything about farming conditions realizes that such changes cannot be put through in a ten-year period without tremendous difficulty and acute suffering to the people who are involved. But by making these adjustments to changed conditions, farmers did get their industry reorganized on a new basis which was setting them slowly but solidly on the road toward economic recovery. The cash income of agriculture was back by 1928 and 1929 to approximately ten billion dollars annually. This was a splendid gain over the seven- and eight-billion-dollar years of 1921 and 1922 and makes a fairly favorable comparison even with the war-time peak if we make allowance for the decline in the level of general prices between 1919 and 1929. Likewise, agricultural income just before the depression was considerably above the pre-war average. While there was still a heavy burden of mortgage debt and increased taxes to be met, there was every reason in 1929 for the farmer to believe that he had built solidly, block on block, a foundation upon which he could proceed to rear in time a structure of permanent prosperity.

Writing in the early fall of 1929, the Secretary of Agriculture said:

> Agricultural conditions in the United States continue gradually to improve. Farm incomes in the crop season 1928–29 averaged higher than those of any season since 1920–21, except 1925–26. The movement of population from the country to the town declined, and the rate of depression in farm-land values declined also. This is evidence of improvement in basic conditions . . . . and there are prospects of continued improvement.

A year later, commenting on these expectations of better prices and higher agricultural income, he said: "All such expectations had to be abandoned with the break in the business situation and the subsequent marked decline in prices." Just as the farmer was beginning to think he had won to a position of safety, he has been engulfed by a tidal wave of melting prices and general financial liquidation which has cut the ground from under his feet.

I do not agree with those who hold that this general price collapse has come as a result of, or by contagion from, the depressed conditions of agriculture. I am quite aware that agriculture cannot be left out of the general picture, and that agricultural troubles have all along been a complicating factor in the foreign situation and an acute aggravating influence once the depression was under way. I am aware also that the wheat industry is sick and with no prospect of early recovery. But to charge farmers with any important measure of responsibility for the crash of 1929 and the severe depression which followed in its train is only another manifestation of the human desire to "pass the buck."

We are often presented with lurid pictures of an economic world swamped by the overproduction of the farmers. Statistics tell us, however, that world-production of the five principal cereals rose only 7.7 per cent from the five-year pre-war average to the level of 1927, 1928, and 1929, and cotton rose only 14.2 per cent. During this period the population of the world rose 10.2 per cent, and that of North and South America, Europe, and Australasia (the production and marketing areas of chief significance for our farmers) rose 13.5 per cent. We must remember that there has been an apparent decline in per capita consumption of cereals as a result of changing food habits, and a sharp decline in demand for horse feed in certain countries with the coming of trucks and tractors. Even so, it does not appear that the agricultural industry was producing any great surplus above the needs of the world if even pre-war living standards were to be maintained. For the welfare of the world it is important that farmers continue producing on approximately this scale (except, probably, in the case of wheat), but it is also vitally important that other classes bring forward a proportionate supply of their goods and services to exchange for the farmer's wares.

Let us leave monetary considerations out of the picture for a moment and sketch in barest outline the farmer's part in the general economic process prior to the collapse of 1929. He was producing an abundant supply of food and raw materials at prices disproportionately low as compared with the general price level. He was contributing an unprecedented tonnage of revenue freight to the railroads, a larger than normal volume of business to the middleman who handled his product, cheap and abundant supplies of raw material to packers, millers, spinners, and other processors of his commodities. So far as his particular responsibility in the economic teamwork of the nation was concerned, he was putting up a good performance. For this, his money reward was, on the average, very meager, and, over large areas, his capital values were shrinking so fast as to carry away not merely any exceptional gains made out of war-time prosperity but even the savings of a generation. Farm people took a lot of punishment. But to say that their troubles were pushing the economic life of the nation to the brink of catastrophe is wide of the mark.

In the long run, economic prosperity and progress depend upon having cheap and abundant raw materials produced by as small a proportion of the population as possible. Thus a larger supply of wealth and human labor are made available to build on this foundation a superstructure of fabricating industries, personal services, and so-called leisure callings. But, if such resources, under the direction of business executives and financiers, are so administered as to create speculative activity, promotional maladjustment of one part of the system to another, and the dissipation of capital unwisely invested, then the whole system breaks down more or less completely.

Now, the critical factor in this whole process is to be found at the point where economic activities translate themselves into financial expression. Bankers and brokers, business executives in their rôle of financial managers of their respective corporations, play a decisive part in determining whether the business world will continue in good health or be permitted or encouraged to follow such a course as will lead to illness of one sort or another. Likewise, legislators and government officials, in acting upon questions of tariff; restrictive, protective, or promotional measures with reference to business; and laws touching currency and banking, have a substantial effect.

I am not as much disposed as some people are to think that there has been very serious misdirection of business activity in the post-war period—that is, as far as the actual process of technical production is concerned. But in terms of the financial management of this private business and of the financial management of public business at home and abroad, we have shown ourselves seriously inept at meeting the difficult and challenging problems which have come in the train of the World War. Until this financial organization within which the economic organization must function has been overhauled and readjusted, it is idle to talk of any thoroughgoing and permanent recovery of general business. And until general business creates a situation of full employment, profitable operation, and free exchange of goods, the farmer's market will be cramped and unsatisfactory.

There are several million people in the United States who want to go back to work so that they can get money to spend in the satisfaction of their desires. There are tens of millions of people in the world as a whole who are in the same situation. Until the general financial and industrial system is again put in good enough running order so that this desire to work may be gratified, purchasing power will be low and business depression will continue. The farmer will slowly adjust himself to this condition by curtailing production and accepting a lower standard of living. Such a solution of the problem would cast enduring discredit on the ability of the present leaders of the world to administer a modern economic society built on the capitalistic pattern. The only tolerable solution will be to straighten out the financial tangles so as to permit the economic process to get into full tide of operation again, making a market capable of absorbing even the present farm output at remunerative prices. Only so will the rest of the world take advantage of the wealth which agriculture is pouring into its lap.

WAGES IN RELATION TO ECONOMIC RECOVERY

Leo Wolman

AN IMPARTIAL wage board, hearing a request for reductions in the wages of building-trades workers in San Francisco a month ago, decided that the wage scale then in force should remain in effect during the year 1932 and thereafter until the occasion arises for its revision. Among the arguments made before this board was the assertion that lowered wages would stimulate building and increase employment. To this the board replied that "no evidence was presented that even a small amount of building is being held up pending a reduction in wages." In addition the board found that "workers have suffered such a drastic reduction in earnings through unemployment as to offset many times any gain they may have made through the reduction in the cost of living." Finally the board held that increased efficiency, "due to improved production on the part of workers, has lowered construction labor costs far more than any reduction that could come from decreasing wage rates."

Two years ago it would have been difficult to find

in this country even so hesitant an admission of the possible need under certain conditions for wage reductions as is contained in this decision of an arbitration board. If, during our last period of prosperity, we had any wage theory at all, it was to the effect that high and rising wages were necessary to a full flow of purchasing power and, therefore, to good business. During the first year of this depression, indeed, business leaders were still saying that "reducing the income of labor is not a remedy for business depression, it is a direct and contributing cause"; or "in this enlightened age when it is recognized that production is dependent upon consuming power, it is my judgment that large manufacturers and producers will maintain wages and salaries as being the farsighted and in the end the most constructive thing to do."

So deeply imbedded was this doctrine of high wages in our national thinking, that the largest of our industries resisted wage cuts until the end of the second year of the depression. Although wages were reduced by many small firms in the highly competitive textile and coal industries from the very beginnings of bad business, the large firms in our basic steel, public-utility, and construction industries publicly announced their adherence to a policy of high wages and their unwillingness to reduce prevailing standards. On the American railroads, the first serious efforts to reduce wages were not made until the fall of 1931. It is indeed impossible to recall any past depression of similar intensity and duration in which the wages of prosperity were maintained as long as they have been during the depression of 1930–31.

This does not mean, of course, that workingmen and women in the United States are earning as much now as they did in 1929. Such a conclusion is obviously absurd. There are, first, some seven millions of unemployed who are not earning anything at all and who subsist on the gifts of charity. The rest, those who are at work, have had their incomes drastically reduced by full unemployment and short time, on the one hand, and by reductions in their wages, on the other. Building-trades labor, for example, pretends that it is still being paid in accordance with its 1929 scale of wages, but everyone knows that where the pressure for jobs is so great labor will gladly work for less. In addition to these reductions in their wage rates, building labor may be conservatively estimated to be unemployed during 1931 at least 25 per cent of the time. The income of a building laborer, therefore, is easily 30 to 40 per cent less in 1931 than in 1929. This picture is typical of the whole of American industry. It has, in fact, been carefully estimated that the total wage and salary bill of this country, excluding public service, is approximately 35 per cent lower in 1931 than in 1929. The greater part of this drop is, however, due to unemployment and the remainder to reductions in wages.

(74)

Where belief in high wages is as strong as it apparently was in this country, what is responsible for the growing pressure for wage reductions since the middle of 1931? For it is now quite plain that American business men, with rare and peculiar exceptions, see in wage reductions a large part of the solution of their present difficulties and, in this respect, have experienced a radical change of heart and mind.

The answer to this difficult question can be had only by understanding the more significant characteristics of the present depression. It is first a depression of long duration; it is already approaching its third year. And it is also a depression marked by a continuous and drastic drop in prices. The longer a depression lasts, the more difficult it becomes for business men and industries to adjust themselves to more and more unfavorable conditions. While some individuals and some industries are better off than others at various stages of the depression, sooner or later all of them are forced by the shrinkage in business to seek new sources of economy, to reduce their overhead charges, to cut dividends—in short to make their business live within its means. If to the shrinkage in the volume of business, there are added the effects of falling prices, the problems of business become more serious and their adjustment to prevailing conditions involves the application of the most drastic of measures.

The railroad industry in this country is a case in point. During the early stages of the depression, when the total volume of business had not yet seriously declined, railroad companies appeared well able to meet and solve their problems. With the prolongation of bad business, however, the face of things changes. Railroad income now suffers not only from the effects of the general depression of business but also from the inroads of the competition of cheaper forms of transport. Meanwhile accumulated reserves and surpluses were exhausted to meet current requirements. Failure to continue expenditures for maintenance and renewal of plant leads rapidly to the deterioration of equipment and services. Dividend reductions and difficulty in earning fixed interest charges tend to impair the credit of railroad companies and to make difficult the renewal of short-term loans. Very soon, then, the railroad companies, burdened under the weight of these problems, are forced by circumstances to seek further savings in their costs of operation and they turn, as they did in November, 1931, to a demand for a general reduction in wages. This picture of the state of affairs in the railroad industry is in substance typical of all industry in the advanced stages of business depression.

The demand for wage cuts, then, represents the inevitable attempt of business to stem the tide of losses. Before this force of falling prices and declining volume of business the individual business man is helpless and he must find his savings wherever he can, and one source of savings is unquestionably wages. This total process of adjusting wages and other costs to prices, of adjusting the prices of one industry to another, and of adjusting wholesale to retail prices, many professional economists regard as essential to the hastening of business recovery.

On the soundness of this view, there is now, as there has always been, sharp difference of opinion. And it is with reference to this divergence of views that the conflict over the validity of the policies of wage reductions has often been fought.

It is the contention of those who oppose wage cutting that the practice of yielding to price decline by setting in train a further decline in prices, through the reduction of labor and other costs, is in itself a dangerous and uncontrollable procedure. Deflation, which is one phase of price decline, is a cumulative process. It spreads from industry to industry and from one economic institution to another. Innumerable illustrations of the process are to be found in the present depression. The drop in prices affects the earnings of companies; poor earnings in turn influence the investors' judgment as to security values; the decline in security values impairs the collateral accounts of banks; banks, moved by the reduced earnings of their borrowers and by the drop in stock prices, become more cautious in the renewal of old and the granting of new credits; the holder of investment funds, finally, uncertain as to the future and predicting a still further decline in current values, holds back his funds and waits until the future is clear.

The huge social cost of this method of achieving business recovery is known to every observer of contemporary events. Several times in the course of the present depression we have been on the verge of financial and business panic. We have exposed ourselves to country-wide bank failures in which the purchasing power of tens of thousands are still tied up. After two years of this sort of thing it is still not evident that the deflation has spent its force. Any substantial resumption of deflation and price cutting may easily again precipitate us into additional bank failures and the insidious undermining of public confidence which inevitably means prolongation of business depression and the resort to more deflation.

To those, then, who see wage cutting and deflation in these terms, the "essential problem is the avoidance of further deflation" and the return to higher prices of the past. If the goal of business recovery is to be approached through the medium of deliberate policy, designed first to arrest the fall in prices and, next, to raise their level, then the alternatives of wage and price cutting are only temporary devices, to be employed in the absence of direct and constructive policies of business revival.

Measures of industrial control alone can prevent reductions in prices and in wages. If the deflation of American values continues at its present pace,

WAGES AND ECONOMIC RECOVERY

then wages together with all other prices and costs will keep on falling. We have already, in the past two years, witnessed the dangers and uncertainties of such deflation. If we are to avoid them in the immediate future, we must prepare ourselves to try the type of experiment in business control which has already commended itself to many of the business leaders of the country. The Swope plan, the proposal for industrial planning made by the United States Chamber of Commerce, and the industrial council of Senator La Follette are nothing more nor less than substitutes for the procedure of deflation, which unavoidably involves price reductions and the cutting of wages.

BANKING POLICIES IN RELATION
TO RECOVERY

JACOB H. HOLLANDER

IT WAS common among the economists of the
Victorian period to refer to banking problems
as the most difficult in the whole field of political economy. On the other hand, an eminent scien-
tist, the lamented Simon Newcomb, was fond of
saying that the principles of monetary science could
be grasped by a child of twelve. I believe firmly that
this is the case.

I am concerned with the present—not with the
past; with banking policies and recovery—not depression. A postmortem is tempting. It permits the
wisdom of hindsight, and the satisfaction of "I told
you so." But the result is barren as to the task at
hand.

The future historian of American banking policies
and practice in the decade just ended will find among
much to praise, something to blame. He will question whether in the buoyant optimism of the reck-
less twenties, American banking was not measurably sucked into the speculative maelstrom; whether

a class of adventuring spirits, whose proper field lay in hazardous enterprise, were not permitted to engage in banking operations. He will ask whether the epidemic of bank mergers and branch extensions did not serve to mask past indiscretions or to gratify personal ambitions or to permit promotion gains. He will indict the injection of political job-filling, and sometimes worse, into state banking examination; and he will condemn the failure to segregate, or at least more adequately to protect, savings deposits as against commercial deposits. He is likely to challenge banking tolerance of pool operations on the stock and produce exchanges; and he will subject to the severest scrutiny the policies of the Federal Reserve banks in relation to international finance as against domestic requirement.

If we turn, however, as we should, from the past to the present and, cautiously, to the future, as to banking policies in relation to economic recovery, it is important to bear two facts in mind:

The first is the vital part that banks and banking practices play, and must play, in the economic life of the country. There can be no business recovery, there can be no widespread economic well-being, unless the banks exercise and exercise efficiently that rôle which a complex economic order assigns them.

The second is that banks are administered by bankers, and that bankers are after all mere men; not economic illiterates, as an eminent member of the fraternity stigmatized them a generation ago, nor on the other hand supermen free from the weaknesses and frailties of human kind. They are "warmed and cooled by the same winter and summer" as other men. The bankers of the United States aspire to be the elect of the business world, outstanding in integrity, capacity, and sobriety. But this is counsel of perfection. The public mind must never be lulled into a blind security. Regulative authority must never forego its vigilant sovereignty. By and large, a country will have a banking system and a banking personnel as good as but no better than it deserves.

The American citizen comes into direct contact with the banks of his country in three ways: He keeps the margin of his income over his expenditure in a savings account; he borrows money for his business and has a deposit and checking account at a commercial bank; and he lives, moves, and has his being in an economic world shaped and determined by the Reserve banks. Savings banks, commercial banks, Reserve banks, are the three essential parts of the American banking structure.

Each of these will play its part in our impending economic recovery.

Savings banks and the savings departments of other banks serve the economic life of the country in a dual capacity. They provide the channel through which an important part of surplus revenue —the excess of individual income over expenditure—drains into a central pool. Into this flow the penny savings of school children, the self-denying provision for the rainy day of modest households, the thrifty economies of the better circumstanced. And, on the other hand, it is from out of this pool of saved income, by the purchase of investment securities, that the savings banks supply the productive enterprises of the country with necessary capital for plant construction and expansion. Both of these activities must function in their accustomed way if the country is to regain a healthy economic life. Should the savings of the country be diverted by withdrawal and hoarding from productive use into barren idleness, there is starvation of plant, delay in business resumption, and aggravation of disquiet and fear.

A no less grave obligation rests upon the savings banks to see to it that funds accumulated and accumulating are promptly set to work. An undue fearsomeness that hoards uninvested funds, a trader-like opportunism that delays bond buying for more favorable market terms, alike retard the return of healthy capital building. When the country's savings flow normally, not excessively, into its savings banks, and when its savings banks resume their traditionally conservative course of bond buying and investing, then the country will have taken the first decisive step toward business recovery. Thereafter it will be proper for public policy to consider and determine whether the practice of protecting savings deposits by special safeguard as to invest-

(83)

ment—exemplified in the case of premier mutual savings banks—shall not be given wider extension by a definite segregation and defense.

The commercial banks of the United States are a vast aggregate of some twenty-five thousand national banks, state banks, trust companies, private banks—scattered over the length and breadth of the land, ranging from the billion-dollar colossi of the metropolis to the little ten-thousand-dollar institutions of placid villages. The prime services they render, widely different in degree, are much the same in kind. The manufacturer, the merchant, the farmer, the citizen makes use of his "bank" as a place for the safe custody of funds, either in his possession or coming to him by remittance or sale, and disbursable at his convenience by check or withdrawal. He goes to his bank to anticipate by loan or discount the value of an incomplete economic performance—the partly finished product of his factory, the marketable but unsold merchandise on his shelves, the unharvested crops in his field. More than this, if he be a man of competence and character, he may reasonably count upon the bank to supplement, from out its unemployed funds or its elastic credit, his own supply of circulating capital when a seasonal expansion presses upon him.

In these past months the commercial banks have, at considerable cost and with some fatalities, extricated themselves from the jam in which a nationwide speculative debauch had caught them. With the subsidence of panicky withdrawal of deposits and hoarding of currency and the return of impounded circulating medium to proper channels, the banks have been able to resume a normal cash position. The operation, indeed the mere organization, of President Hoover's admirably conceived National Credit Corporation has given secondary reserves a potential liquidity, and diverted the need of demoralizing security sales. Best of all, with growing business hopefulness—the forerunner of positive recovery—the commercial assets of the banks, for months if not frozen at least congealed, are steadily thawing in the warming glow of returning sunshine.

This is convalescence. Instead of "save who can," the slogan of American banking is today—"Beyond the Alps lies Italy!" There will be no stampede into a false stride. Wounds, some of them more than skin-deep, will heal. At least some measure of past experience will adhere.

But the curves move upward! The commercial banks have put their households in order. With faith in the resources of the United States, in the resourcefulness of its people, they stand ready in sobriety and courage to organize and advance the forces making for economic recovery.

The field marshalship of American banking resides in these days more than ever in the Reserve banks. When in 1914 our banking system—or *un*-system— passed from irresponsible decentralization to organized leadership, guerilla operations in time of need were replaced by staff direction. It is an old legal dictum that "where the gift, there the burden." There is in the whole range of American financial endeavor no more brilliant performance than the activities of the Federal Reserve banks in these past seventeen years. Errors may have been committed, opportunities may have been lost—but, in my opinion, it is an incompetent and jaundiced attitude to withhold the highest praise for what has been done.

Stern days still lie ahead. To hold the balance between international service and domestic requirement; to encourage enterprise without fanning speculation; to guide without controlling; to do much without begetting the belief that it can do all— these are the tasks of the Reserve system.

In confidence and cheer, American banking faces the dawn!

FORWARD PLANNING OF PUBLIC WORKS TO STABILIZE EMPLOYMENT

Otto T. Mallery

AN OCEAN liner was launched the other day with a new stabilizing device to prevent rolling. It has rapidly rotating wheels, called gyroscopic stabilizers, which keep the ship steady no matter how high the waves. If Columbus could sail his ship now, equipped with this stabilizer, he would hardly know the same old ocean.

What if we could develop such stabilizing devices for industry and employment? What if we could prevent millions of men being rolled out of their jobs every five or ten years by economic storms like the present? Somehow this must be done. The American spirit rebels against the insoluble. Some window must open out on a better prospect.

The simplest way to begin is on some one industry first. Stabilize one ship at a time and one industry at a time. The inventor of the stabilizer for the new liner did not begin by trying to stabilize the ocean.

The construction industry is a good beginning. It is big enough and unstable enough. The outlay for

(87)

construction in 1928 was over $9,000,000,000, or one and one-half times the output of the vast iron and steel industry. You will get a good picture of its magnitude if you imagine all the industrious cows and reliable hens doing their utmost and still not producing half as much value as public works, in spite of the fact that their output is double the value of all the grain crops. The construction industry is at present most unstable. It has fallen in 1931, just when we needed to have it rise, to about one-half its peak during the prosperous year 1928. The first step in stabilizing it, and through it other industries, is through that part of it which is called public works.

What we are about to consider sounds so simple and natural that you will gladly accept it. The proposal is that each governmental unit, such as towns, counties, states, should plan their public works for six years ahead instead of for one year as at present. Then when a period of unemployment occurs, each government could do much more than one year's work, much more than one-sixth of the six-year total. In a year of unemployment let each town vigorously catch up with past and present needs for public improvements. This policy is often called the "prosperity reserve" because it reserves some borrowing power, some public work, and some prosperity for bad times. This sounds simple and easy, but it is not.

We are playing for great stakes, for public works

provides about one-third of the total outlay for construction. To put it a different way, public works equals one-half the outlay for private construction. Public works is a big employer, employing directly about 900,000 men. Towns, great and small, do most of it. The federal government usually does less than 10 per cent of it, but this year has expanded to about 20 per cent of the total. Doesn't it surprise you to find that a year's outlay on public works is often four times the proceeds of the wheat crop with wheat at a dollar a bushel? Assuming that one-half the cost of public works is for labor on the job and for labor in making the materials, then public works wages in an active year have been about one and one-quarter times the wages paid to all hired labor on all the farms of the country. Evidently public works is a giant worth harnessing to the public good.

Will Rogers, a good guide to public opinion, says: "We ought to have advance plans in case of depression just as we do in case of fire. Walk, don't run, to the nearest exit." Everybody agrees in times like the present but nobody does anything about it after the skies clear. That is the trouble, for public works cannot be quickly improvised and expanded after bad times have arrived. An absolute essential is advance planning over at least a six-year period. Therefore the towns and cities, in spite of valiant efforts, have been able to show in the aggregate little if any increase in their public works during 1931.

Disappointment is keen that the hopeful talk and impressive figures we have all heard have not materialized.

The federal government has done better because it had started long-range planning on its own account. The federal government appropriations for roads in 1931 are more than twice the average for the past ten years. The estimated federal expenditures for all kinds of public works, including post-offices and river and harbor improvements, for the calendar year 1931 are $725,000,000, or about three times that of the boom year of 1928. This is the best record ever made by the federal government in expanding public works during any depression. Many think it should do still better.

Even this great federal effort will be found at the end of the year not to have offset, in all probability, the fall in the volume of public works by towns and cities. What did your town do? Why did it not do more? If you look into this, as I hope you will, you may find that the reasons are, first, no long-range plans, and, second, no reserve of borrowing power.

Did your town sell so many bonds for public works during good times that it had few left to sell this year? This is one of the snags in our proposal, one of the monkey wrenches that wreck the economic machinery. A large outstanding bonded debt causes a high tax rate in good times, and what was a high tax in good times is dangerously high in bad times. The town cannot then safely sell any bonds for public works when unemployment is worst. Such a town is like a bank that keeps no reserves and fails in an emergency. The town is bankrupt in ability to give work to its citizens when they need it most. One way to avoid this helplessness is long-range budgeting of bond issues. This means that after estimating the available borrowing power for the next six years some part of it is earmarked and reserved for unemployment emergencies. This takes good management.

The other day I heard a banker say: "It is absurd to ask a town to do public works under conditions like the present, when its taxes don't even take care of running expenses." True enough. But what put the town in that condition? What it did in good times, or what bad times did to it? Often the high taxes, high expenditures, and large bond issues for public works at high prices during boom times caused the trouble that only comes to light in the crucial test of bad times. Towns often go broke in good times but not until bad times does the truth come out. Therefore bad times get the blame rather than bad management. Advance budgeting of bond issues over a six-year period will help to keep a town solvent both in good times and bad.

You have heard people say that public works helps only the construction laborer. Are they not mistaken? Does it not help the storekeeper and the factory worker? The public works worker spends his wages with the storekeeper. His wages also create a demand for shoes and stockings, as one example, and send factory workers back to the factory to make more shoes and stockings. The wages of these shoe and stocking workers create a demand for more milk, garments, radios, and everything else. Next the workers in the twenty-seven industries that produce construction materials also get more wages. They in turn spend more at the five-and-ten-cent stores, for instance, which buy more from a hundred different kinds of factories, which in turn employ more people.

The flow of all this new business is like the circulation of blood in the body. No one can trace the course of each drop but it eventually reaches every part of the body. The fingers cannot tell where the circulating blood started. The vigorous prosecution of public works in any part of the country is like a strong heart beat circulating activity into the remotest extremities of the business structure of the whole country. A hardware house made a fortune by tracing the connection between a good apple crop and the demand for manicure sets. The house instructed its one hundred traveling salesmen to report each county in grain territory where the apple crop was promising. Then it shipped manicure sets and kitchen utensils to the local hardware stores, because it knew that the wife would have the apple money as her perquisite and would satisfy her needs rather than those of the men. In the same way a good crop of public works creates a demand for unexpected kinds of goods of many sorts, not merely construction labor.

But public works is not stimulating employment on a large scale today because few towns and cities have advance plans or reserves of borrowing power. Had we these two missing helpers public works could be expanded in periods of falling prices, which deter a private employer from producing goods he could not sell at a profit should prices continue falling. The lower the price, the better for the community that pays the bills. Therefore the more public works a community executes in a time of depression and the less it executes during boom periods, the lower will be the total ten-year cost of its improvements. Nothing is so expensive for a community as the cost of *not* planning in advance.

Public works also differs from most other commodities in that it does not have to be paid for out of current wages and incomes. But the goods in the department store windows do have to be paid for out of current wages and incomes. There is no use trying to sell furniture in volume when the volume of current wage payments is low. Public works, on the contrary, being largely financed by bond issues, are paid for out of the communities' taxes for the next thirty years or so, including many years of prosperity. This is as it should be, because these new roads, bridges, sewers, etc., will be giving service for many years to come and should be paid for in part by those who will enjoy their future use.

The sale of bonds puts more money into circulation, which is the chief need during a depression. For the total money in circulation today (and by money we include bank deposits, commercial paper, etc.) is much less than during previous prosperous years. The sale of public works bonds during a depression, by increasing the money in circulation, helps to prevent the price-level of commodities from falling.

Fortunately the market for sound municipal bonds is today as good or better than for any other class of investments, doubtless because municipal bonds are one of the safest forms of investment. During much of a depression a well-managed town could not only buy the materials for public works for less, but could also borrow the money at a lower rate of interest than during boom years. The economy is apparent.

The chief obstacles lie in municipal administration, but they can be overcome. Here is a challenge to public service for you and for citizens in a hundred other towns. Find out what changes and planning are needed in your town to do more public works in bad times and less in boom times when everything costs more. The knowledge is available. You may inquire of your library or of the University of Chicago Press, which has published a reading guide for the subject of this lecture and others in the Economic Series. You may write to the new Federal Employment Stabilization Board, Department of Commerce, Washington, and ask what the federal government is doing in the way of making six-year advance construction plans. Perhaps the Federal Employment Stabilization Board will give you suggestions for your town.

You can stabilize your town, like the new ocean liner with its anti-rolling device, and make employment safer and steadier. When such planning has been adopted by most of the towns and states a release of a federal public works program at the advent of a business recession will be a signal for a general release of construction reserves. Then one step will have been taken to curb the extreme fluctuations of nation-wide unemployment. On that day each of us can face the future with greater security.

BIBLIOGRAPHY

TITLES OF GENERAL INTEREST

Clay, Henry, *Economics for the General Reader.* Macmillan, 1918.
Edie, Lionel D., *Economics: Principles and Problems.* Crowell, 1926.
Einzig, Paul, *The World Economic Crisis.* Macmillan, 1931.
Paish, Sir George, *Way to Recovery.* Putnam, 1931.
Patterson, Ernest M., *World's Economic Dilemma.* McGraw-Hill, 1930.
Slichter, Sumner H., *Modern Economic Society.* Holt, 1931.
Taussig, Frank W., *Principles of Economics.* (3rd ed.) Macmillan, 1921.
Academy of Political Science, New York, *Depression and Revival.* A series of addresses and papers presented at the semi-annual meeting, April 24, 1931 (Proceedings, Vol. XIV, No. 3). The Academy, 1931.
Conference on Unemployment, Washington, D.C., 1921. Committee on Recent Economic Changes. *Recent Economic Changes in the United States.* McGraw-Hill, 1929.

I. FORERUNNERS OF THE PRESENT DEPRESSION

Burton, Theodore E., *Financial Crises and Periods of Industrial and Commercial Depression.* Appleton, 1902.
Lightner, Otto C., *The History of Business Depressions.* The Northeastern Press, *c.* 1922.
Mitchell, Wesley C., *Business Cycles: The Problem and Its Setting.* National Bureau of Economic Research, 1927.
Persons, Warren M., *Forecasting Business Cycles.* J. Wiley and Sons, 1931.
Pigou, Arthur C., *Industrial Fluctuations.* (2nd ed.) Macmillan, 1930.
Sprague, O. M. W., *History of Crises under the National Banking System.* Government Printing Office, 1910. (U.S. 61st Cong. 2d Sess. Senate Doc. 538.)

II. SOCIAL ASPECTS OF THE DEPRESSION

Beveridge, Sir William, *Unemployment, a Problem of Industry.* Longmans, 1930.
Calkins, Clinch, *Some Folks Won't Work.* Harcourt, 1930.

Carroll, Mollie R., *Unemployment Insurance in Germany*. The Brookings Institution, 1929.
Davison, Ronald C., *Unemployed, Old Policies and New*. Longmans, 1929.
Douglas, Paul H., and Director, Aaron, *The Problem of Unemployment*. Macmillan, 1931.
Morley, Felix, *Unemployment Relief in Great Britain*. Houghton, 1924.
National Federation of Settlements, Unemployment Committee, *Case Studies of Unemployment*. Press of the Univ. of Pennsylvania, 1931.

III. America and the Balance Sheet of Europe

Angell, James W., *The Recovery of Germany*. Yale Univ. Press, 1929.
Culbertson, William S., *International Economic Policies*. Appleton, 1925.
Moulton, Harold G., and McGuire, C. E., *Germany's Capacity to Pay*. McGraw-Hill, 1923.
Moulton, Harold G., and Pasvolsky, Leo, *World War Debt Settlements*. Macmillan, 1926.
Myers, Denys P., *The Reparation Settlement, 1930*. World Peace Foundation, 1930.
Papers and Proceedings of the American Economic Association, 1929.
Schaacht, Hjalmar, *The End of Reparations*. J. Cape and H. Smith, 1931.

IV. International Economic Interdependence

Buell, Raymond, *International Relations*. (Rev. ed.) Holt, 1929.
Donaldson, John, *International Economic Relations*. Longmans, 1928.
Feis, Herbert, *Europe the World's Banker, 1870–1914*. Yale Univ. Press, 1930.
Nourse, Edwin G., *American Agriculture and the European Market*. The Brookings Institution, 1924.
Wallace, Benjamin B., and Edminster, L. R., *International Control of Raw Materials*. The Brookings Institution, 1930.

V. Effects of Depressions upon Employment and Wages

Butler, H. B., *Unemployment Problems in the United States*. World Peace Foundation, 1931.
Clay, Henry, *Post-War Unemployment Problems*. Macmillan, 1929.
Douglas, Paul H., *Real Wages in the United States, 1890–1926*. Mifflin, 1930.
Douglas, Paul H., and Director, A., *The Problem of Unemployment*. Macmillan, 1931.

Hobson, John A., *Economics of Unemployment*. Macmillan, 1923.
King, W. I., *The National Income and Its Purchasing Power*. National Bureau of Economic Research, 1930.
King, W. I., *Employment Hours and Earnings in Prosperity and Depression—United States 1920–1922*. National Bureau of Economic Research, 1923.
Lauck, William J., *New Industrial Revolution and Wages*. Funk, 1929.
National Industrial Conference Board, *Wages in the United States, 1914–1930*. National Industrial Conference Board, 1931.
President's Conference on Unemployment, *Recent Economic Changes in the United States*. McGraw-Hill, 1929. (Chap. xii.)

VI. BUSINESS DEPRESSIONS AND BUSINESS PROFITS

Donham, Wallace B., *Business Adrift*. McGraw-Hill, 1931.
Hawtrey, Ralph G., *Trade and Credit*. Longmans, 1928.
Thorp and Mitchell, *Business Annals*. National Bureau of Economic Research, 1926.
Young, Richard D., "Profits in American Industry," *American Bankers Association Journal*, September, 1931, Vol. 24, 1, pp. 134–35, 184.
Conference on Unemployment, Washington, D.C., 1921, *Business Cycles and Unemployment*. McGraw-Hill, 1923.
Data Compiled by Industrial Service Department, First National Bank in St. Louis, from published corporation statements.

VII. AGRICULTURE IN RELATION TO ECONOMIC RECOVERY

Black, John D., *Agricultural Reform in the United States*. McGraw-Hill, 1929.
International Institute of Agriculture, *Agricultural Situation in 1929 and 1930*. Economic Commentary on the International Yearbook of Agricultural Statistics for 1929–30. Rome.
League of Nations, Economic Committee, *The Agricultural Crisis*. World Peace Foundation, 1931.
International Conference of Agricultural Economists, *Proceedings of the Second International Conference of Agricultural Economists*. George Banta Pub. Co., 1930.

VIII. WAGES IN RELATION TO ECONOMIC RECOVERY

Cole, G. D. H., *Payment of Wages*, Allen & Unwin, 1918.
Dobb, Maurice H., *Wages*. Harcourt, 1928.

BIBLIOGRAPHY

Friday, David, *Profits, Wages, and Prices.* Harcourt, 1920.

Pigou, Arthur C., *Industrial Fluctuations.* (2nd ed.) Macmillan, 1930.

IX. BANKING POLICIES IN RELATION TO RECOVERY

Cassel, Gustav, *Post-War Monetary Stabilization.* Columbia Univ. Press, 1928.

Edie, Lionel D., *Capital, the Money Market, and Gold.* Univ. of Chicago Press, 1929.

Laughlin, J. Laurence, *New Exposition of Money, Credit, and Prices.* Univ. of Chicago Press, 1931.

League of Nations, Financial Committee, *Reports of the Gold Delegation.* World Peace Foundation, 1930-31.

Owens, Richard N., and Hardy, C. O., *Interest Rates and Stock Speculation.* Macmillan, 1925.

X. FORWARD PLANNING OF PUBLIC WORKS

Conference on Unemployment, Washington, D.C., 1921. Committee on Recent Economic Changes. *Planning and Control of Public Works.* National Bureau of Economic Research, 1930.

Davison, R. C., *The Unemployed.* Longmans, 1929.

Foster, William T., and Catchings, Waddill, *The Road to Plenty.* Houghton, 1928.

International Labor Office, *Unemployment and Public Works.* World Peace Foundation, Boston, Mass, 1931.

Loucks, William N., *The Stabilization of Employment in Philadelphia through the Long Range Planning of Municipal Improvement Projects.* University of Pennsylvania Press, 1931.

McMurry, Donald L., *Coxey's Army.* Little Brown and Co.

Mallery, Otto T., *Public Works and Unemployment, a Plan for the United States.* In preparation.

Wolman, Leo., *Planning and Control of Public Works.* National Bureau of Economic Research, 1930.

(99)

PROPOSED ROADS TO ECONOMIC RECOVERY

GOLD, INTERNATIONAL TRADE BALANCES, AND PROSPERITY

James Harvey Rogers

IN OPENING this evening the series of addresses on "Proposed Roads to Economic Recovery," it is my task to present to you in the fewest words possible the relations between gold and depression.

Strange as it may seem, the monetary systems of the civilized world were, until very recently, based almost exclusively upon gold—a substance used otherwise solely for ornamentation. Only six months ago it might have been said that the world had become virtually a gold-standard world.

In recent months, however, much has happened to our time-honored monetary systems, hitherto so firmly based on this primitive, savage instinct for adornment.

Last summer, amid a great fanfare of trumpets was announced the so-called "Hoover Moratorium." Thus, in an attempt to safeguard in England and in Germany the highly important gold standard, the President of the United States rightly ended once and for all the persistent fiction that it is possible for this country to maintain a policy of political isolation.

(103)

After much nervousness throughout international banking and credit circles—dramatized by hurried flights from capital to capital by the able and patriotic governor of the Bank of England—the pound sterling ceased to be a gold unit, and London, the financial center of the world.

Still more recently, in the midst of increasing money and credit confusion, of bank failures, of tragic unemployment, and of general business depression, one country after another has been forced off this all-important and generally excellent (though exceedingly strange and little understood) system of values. Indeed, in the brief space of six months, no less than twenty countries—including some of the most highly civilized in the world—have had to surrender the prestige of the monetary system so generally regarded as the best the world has yet found.

What is the gold standard—this mysterious potentate which thus, at least temporarily, seems to be dictating the destinies of even the most powerful? And can any of the frightful evils of the depression from which the world is suffering be traced to his ever present influence? Let us see.

In gold-standard countries, the monetary units are defined as given weights of pure gold. In the United States, for example, the dollar is defined as 23.22 grains of fine gold. Moreover, having been thus defined, careful provision has been made to maintain the definition. If anyone has gold, he may, by taking it to one of the government offices, receive in return dollars, one for each 23.22 grains of fine gold.

If, on the other hand, he has dollars, he may demand gold coins or gold bars in exchange and thus receive 23.22 grains of fine gold for each dollar presented.

In other words, gold and dollars are kept completely interchangeable—23.22 grains of fine gold being kept always interchangeable with one dollar.

Because of this simple but invariable relationship, it follows that the value of this given weight of gold is always exactly equivalent to that of a dollar and vice versa. Whatever happens, therefore, to the value of gold happens automatically to that of the dollar; and whatever happens to the value of the dollar happens equally automatically to the value of gold.

Suppose, for example, that gold should become as plentiful and as cheap as copper, the dollar would become equally cheap and would buy correspondingly little. If, on the other hand, gold were to become greatly in demand without equally great increase in the supply, its value relative to that of other things would rise correspondingly, and so would that of the dollar.

That there is just such a greatly increased demand for gold in the world today and that the supplies available for those needing it most urgently have at the same time become more difficult to obtain, I shall now proceed to show. In fact, among the civilized nations of the world there is a veritable scramble for gold. The drastic price declines from which for more than two years the world has been suffering, are in no uncertain way connected with this scramble.

Of the approximately 400 million dollars worth of gold mined each year, roughly one-half goes into the arts to be made into watches and jewelry and to be used in filling teeth. The other half goes automatically into the monetary gold stock of the world —there to serve as a basis for our money and credit systems. This enormous gold reserve now amounts to a little more than 11 billion dollars—or, if all melted together, to a gold cube thirty-two feet square.

Where, then, you may ask, is there any possible shortage? The answer is: There is no actual shortage for all the gold-standard world taken together, but this huge existing stock is so badly distributed that while, in two countries, large unused supplies lie locked up and idle, in many others there is too little to maintain the standard.

The United States, for example, even after its recent great losses, holds 36 per cent of the world's total and France 22 per cent. England, on the other hand, holds barely 6 per cent and Germany less than 3 per cent. Moreover, a situation very similar to the one just described has existed for several years, with the United States and France claiming an ever larger portion of the total.

The difficulties experienced by a country suffering from a gold shortage can perhaps best be described by pointing out those recently confronted by England and by Germany.

In England, during a number of months prior to the collapse of the gold standard, it became more and more generally known that the entire British gold stock was less than enough to pay the short-term credits held in London by Paris bankers alone.

In Germany, at the same time, it became known that the total of foreign short-term credits in the Berlin market was more than five times the gold holdings of the central bank of that country.

Since a great portion of such short-term credits can be withdrawn literally overnight, the danger of being thrown suddenly off the gold standard was continually imminent in both of the countries mentioned. Moreover, in all the big money and investment centers are sold many internationally-held securities. Once a gold standard is threatened, the sale of the securities of the distressed country, and the purchase of those payable in more certainly stable money units, increases the ever more dangerous gold outflow. Under such circumstances, the possibilities of political pressure from abroad are as evident as are the tragic uncertainties in the credit structure and in the securities markets of the threatened country.

The evils of a gold shortage, while often unnoticed until some jolt to international confidence appears, are thus ever present in the form of a threat to economic, to political, and even to diplomatic security. Strenuous and persistent efforts, therefore, are made to remove them.

The quickest and often the easiest way to build up a waning gold reserve is, through central bank action, to stimulate a rise in short-term interest rates. Funds are thus attracted from abroad and usually bring with them a gold inflow. In periods of stress, however, when confidence has already been shaken, not only does such a device often fail to bring the expected relief, but whatever relief is thus found intensifies the threat of short-term credit withdrawal.

More permanent and immediately less dangerous devices are therefore sought. If exports can be increased relatively to imports much more stable and satisfactory relief is found. Hence strenuous efforts are made to throw all the goods possible on the international markets and to take as few as possible therefrom.

To stimulate exports, bounties and dumping of one sort or another are instituted.

For reducing imports the most ready device is the protective tariff. Moreover, in periods of falling prices like the present, it is especially popular because it gives *apparent* (but usually only apparent) promise of raising directly internal prices at the same time that it attracts gold from abroad. Hence, in the period of our history when international communications have made their greatest advances, the world is fast becoming a collection of walled estates comparable with those of the Dark Ages.

To gain additional control over international trade balances and hence over gold movements, many countries have gone further still. Central banks have been given more and more complete control over the foreign exchanges, and many imports are arbitrarily cut off by a refusal to grant the exchange required for payment.

It is to such vicious and highly damaging medieval policies that the gold scramble, in combination with other influences, is leading. Meanwhile the price level has continued its tragic decline and the business of the world has become more and more depressed.

The relation between falling prices and depression requires but little comment. As business is at present organized, costs in general precede selling prices. If, during the process of production, selling prices so decline as to fail to meet previously incurred costs, profits are automatically turned into losses and many businesses are forced to close.

One other often forgotten influence is of equal importance. Far from being entirely flexible and hence adjustable to changing conditions of all sorts, our price system contains prices of every degree of rigidity. On one end of the scale are those completely flexible, adjusting themselves readily to happenings or even rumors of happenings in any part of the world. On the other end are those of almost complete inflexibility, changing only to meet the rulings of a bankruptcy court. If the price of your product is among the highly flexible ones while your costs—as is frequently the case—are highly inflexible, your profits, in periods of rapidly falling prices, are likewise automatically turned into losses. And the more rapid and more drastic the declines, the greater and more general will the losses be.

Whatever may be said, therefore, as to the so-called causes of the depression, of this we may be confident: *Until the drastic and rapid decline of commodity prices can be at least arrested, business recovery on a broad scale can hardly be anticipated.* In consequence, it is of the utmost importance that effective measures to this end be adopted.

If the scramble for gold is to be relieved, the existing supplies in France and in the United States, where plentiful, will have to be more effectively used. To be more effectively used, measures must be taken to make them support a greater credit and money superstructure.

Very fortunately, our excellent Federal Reserve System provides the machinery for just such measures. Through open-market purchases of bills and of government securities, if maintained courageously and with persistence, these central banking institutions have it within their power to bring early, if only partial, relief.

Such purchases put entirely new funds into the hands of the sellers. If the seller is a banker, he thus increases directly his lending and investing power; if an individual (or firm) he deposits the proceeds in his bank which thus gets a similar though indirect enhancement of its lending position. Even if —as frequently happens—the receiving bank uses the new funds only to pay existing indebtedness at the Federal Reserve bank or with a city correspondent, the enhancement of its lending position and— more important still—of its power to command the confidence of its depositors is just as great. More-over, in a period of disastrous liquidation like the present one, the receipt of such additional funds in the form of new deposits removes for many hard-pressed banks the painful necessity of selling their best and most liquid investments on a weak and declining market.

Through such utilization of powers already theirs can the Federal Reserve banks arrest the present tragic liquidation and halt the disastrous price decline. Such a policy, too, would aid greatly in redistributing the world's monetary gold stocks and in securing again the normal and healthful functioning of the gold standard.

THE TARIFF IN RELATION TO PROSPERITY

ERNEST M. PATTERSON

THOSE of you who have been following this series of radio talks on "Aspects of the Present Depression" must by this time be convinced that a major business depression is a highly complex affair. Its aspects are many, no simple panacea can cure it, and even the economic doctors are disagreeing in some of their diagnoses.

These difficulties are not diminished when we examine the topic of this evening—"The Tariff in Relation to Prosperity." Protective tariffs are old devices, not new ones. At various times they have been employed by all countries. In recent years, there have been only a few countries that have been nominally "free trade" and this winter the most prominent of that small group, Great Britain, is deliberately adopting protective duties. For over a hundred years, our own country has had a protective tariff system, and today the general level of our duties is higher than ever before.

It is easy to understand that tariffs have become a very important part of the world's economic organization. Industries are adjusted to the existing levels of duties. Political policies are affected by the fact that our own country and others have tariffs. Any proposal to lower tariffs brings vigorous protests from those who believe that they would be injured by such a change. In those sections of the country where economic life is greatly dependent on present tariff levels, belief in the efficacy of tariffs assumes an almost religious fervor. Today our two major political parties almost agree in their support of a protective policy.

There is not time this evening to discuss the general issue. Instead, we shall briefly consider the tariff in its relation to our present acute situation. Fortunately, there are few, if any, who will disagree with the statement that no matter what the merits of any commodity or device, an excess of it is possible. King Midas had too much gold. In the play *Brewster's Millions*, the leading character had too much income and had a very unhappy time trying to dispose of it. A medicine, excellent in small doses, may be very harmful if taken in large quantities.

Likewise, there may be excessively high tariffs. Even those who favor protective tariffs will agree, at least after a little thought, that they might be too numerous and too high. A protective tariff has as its purpose the protection of domestic industries against the importation of competing goods from other countries. Its intent is to keep out of the country at least a part of the goods from abroad. Probably no one would argue that tariffs should be so numerous and so high as to keep out all imports from all countries. Certainly none of us would favor having other countries raise their tariffs to a level that would keep out all of the goods that we would like to sell to them.

There are many people who believe that all protective tariffs should be abolished, but even those who favor protection will agree that there is somewhere a limit above which duties cannot be raised without injurious results. Today, tariffs throughout the world have reached or gone far past that limit.

How generally this is felt by experts is illustrated by the report of the World Economic Conference held in Geneva in 1927. Delegates were there from practically all countries in the world, including five very able representatives appointed by the government of the United States. This conference, in a report signed by the American delegates along with the rest, argued that tariffs were too high, their views being summarized in the statement that "the time has come to put an end to the increase in tariffs and to move in the opposite direction."

This was in 1927 and since that time tariff duties have been raised by nearly all important countries, including the United States, which raised its duties in 1930. The latest important additions are those now being made by Great Britain. The movement has gone too far. Trade is being unwisely restrained. Each country is attempting to aid its own economic life, but the result, as characterized by Sir Arthur

Salter, for years the able Director of the Economic and Financial Section of the League of Nations, is "collective suicide."

Some countries claim that there are urgent reasons for their tariffs. The British argue that they have for nearly a hundred years lacked protection and that they are at a serious disadvantage without it. The Germans maintain that they can pay reparations only if they restrict their imports and in every way possible increase their exports.

In the United States we can use neither of these arguments. We have had protective tariffs for over one hundred years. We do not have to pay reparations, nor any other kind of foreign debt. Instead, we are now the great creditor nation of the world. Large amounts are due each year as interest to individual Americans who have invested abroad. Except for the period of the "Hoover Moratorium" on political debts there are due several hundred million dollars each year from several foreign governments to the government of the United States. In addition to this, our exporters wish to sell a large volume of goods abroad each year and in the last analysis the payment must come largely in the form of imported goods.

In a world-wide situation we are thus in a somewhat unique position. If we are to sell our goods abroad in large volume and if we are to receive the amounts due us on the public and private debts, we must receive something. If we do not wish to receive imported goods freely there are just two alternatives open to us. One is to resume the purchase of foreign securities as we were doing from 1924 to 1929. Just now this does not seem to be our desire. Probably the United States will not be a good foreign bond market for some time to come. The other alternative is for us to accept the fact that some of our foreign debtors cannot pay what they owe us. They will default on their obligations and as investors we shall lose. Bankers express the problem by saying that there is a shortage of foreign exchange. This is a serious fact for debtors in many countries who do not wish to default but are anxious to meet their obligations. It is tragic for American investors who have in good faith purchased large quantities of foreign securities. With fewer restrictions on trade much more could be paid on these bonds than can be paid with barriers so high. The people of other countries can pay us only with commodities and the obstacles to commercial intercourse are too numerous. Trade is being choked to death.

Excessive tariffs are by no means the only cause of the present depression, but they are one very serious factor. Yet their elimination or even their moderate reduction is not easy. Many years ago, in one of our presidential campaigns, a cartoon appeared in one of our prominent weekly papers. In it Uncle Sam was shown on a pair of tall stilts. He was high in the air, towering above the trees and the houses in a very perilous position. The stilts were marked "high tariffs." Uncle Sam could find no way of getting down without serious injury.

The cartoon was an excellent one. When tariffs are raised, the particular industries affected adjust themselves to the high duties. Often the removal or lowering of those duties will bring hardship, and we hesitate to take so serious a step. Today, however, we are facing large losses. Within a few post-war years our relation to the rest of the world has abruptly changed and our entire economic structure has been put under severe strain.

We cannot escape all losses. Our task is to minimize them and to distribute them as equitably as possible. Congress, apparently backed by general public opinion, objects to further reductions of the political debts. Private investors insist they wish to be paid what is due them and hesitate to buy more foreign bonds. Exporters declare they must maintain or increase their sales of goods abroad.

Important public questions are usually settled after a conflict between the different groups concerned. There are large numbers of people who gain and still others who believe they gain through our present high import duties. They make their money chiefly by selling goods in the domestic market and they are anxious to keep out of that market the goods of their foreign competitors. High tariffs are to their advantage, at least as they see it.

In recent years two other classes are growing in power. One includes those who are making money by selling goods abroad. Years ago these were chiefly the producers of raw materials, including agricultural products, who could sell with little effort. Today they face much keener competition. In recent years our manufacturers have gone into foreign markets more than in the past and they, too, are finding an increasing difficulty in making sales.

These exporters are coming to realize that people abroad can buy only in case foreign commodities can be sold in the United States. As a result, many of our leading manufacturers and many producers of raw materials are far less enthusiastic in their support of high tariffs than they were a few decades ago, and some of them definitely opposed our tariff of 1930.

The second class whose power is gaining includes all owners of foreign securities and it ought to include all who firmly believe that the debts due to our government by foreign governments should be paid in full. Such payments, too, cannot be made except from the proceeds of foreign imports into the United States. These investors are scattered all over the country and many are people of moderate means.

Between these groups with contradictory interests there will of necessity be a struggle. Those who will gain through a greater freedom of trade are growing in strength and it is probable that they can prevent further increases in our tariff duties. Whether they can bring about actual reductions in the near future is not so clear.

We are in the midst of an impossible situation. If we are to insist on the payment of sums due some way of facilitating payments must be found. We may close by repeating the statement of the World Economic Conference, "the time has come to put an end to the increase in tariffs and to move in the opposite direction." Conditions now are far more acute than four and a half years ago when that statement was made, and we in the United States have more to lose and less to gain than the people of most other countries if we ignore this advice.

WHAT THE CONSUMER SHOULD DO

F. W. Taussig

WHAT should be the attitude of the consumer in the present depression? Can he or she help, by keeping up expenditures, by lessening them, or by increasing them? What is the relation of the consumer's doings to the underlying causes of the depression?

This is the subject of my talk. By way of preliminary I must say a word about the state of our knowledge on the subject at large.

The economists are sadly perplexed by the business depression. The cycles of prosperity and depression are familiar enough, and have been watched and studied by able and competent persons for years. An enormous amount of information has been collected, and there has been steady progress not only toward knowing the facts but toward understanding them. Yet when it comes to stating the cause or causes, we are still on uncertain ground. And when it comes to a program for prevention and remedy, we are on even more uncertain ground.

In one respect, however, we see our way. We understand some of the main *lines* on which the cycles run, and the main lines along which we must proceed. I will just mention some of the important outstanding aspects which we have to consider: money and banking matters; speculation and the psychology of business; international relations and international trade; overproduction or disorganized production. It is the last named of these—disorganized production—that leads also to the problems of consumption. Accordingly it is to this last that I shall hereafter attend. The other lines I shall let alone, not because they are unimportant, but because they are connected much less with our particular subject—the consumer's doings.

One great cause of the depression is that we have *mal*adjustment of production and distribution. Perhaps it would be better to say *disproportioned* production. There is not *over*production, in the sense of there being more produced than people can use. There are not more goods of all kinds than could be sold at some price or other. But there are some goods—a limited list, even though in the aggregate a very considerable one—of which more is produced than can be sold at a profit. This is what is meant by disproportioned production or "malproduction." When it happens, some of the capital and labor which have been directed to making the undue proportion of goods must make a shift. Or else the capital and labor must just sit and wait, be idle or part idle, until in some way the demand catches up with the excess.

The automobile is a familiar illustration. During the boom vast plants were put up, or existing plants enlarged, and hundreds of thousands of workers were employed in making more cars than the people wanted (as it proved in the end) at the prices that would pay the capital and labor their fair or expected rates. The same sort of thing happened with radios, apartments, some kinds of houses, some house supplies—such as plumbing and heating appliances—city office buildings. This was true of wheat, the staff of life, and (at the other extreme) of silk hosiery. Not only so; but industries which turned out materials and supplies for these industries were similarly overdone. Plants were enlarged and equipped for making more sheet steel for the motor manufacturers, more iron and brass pipe for plumbing and heating, more structural steel for skyscrapers, more cement for foundations and walls, more tractors and combines (those marvels among agricultural machinery) for wheat raising. The plant equipment was disproportionate. The maladjustment ramified far.

Now, the direction in which the return to prosperity is to be sought is in the path of readjustment. Let capital and labor be turned toward industries not overdone. Such are the lines of helpful procedure. What can the consumer do along them?

In answering this question we must, of course, have in mind what would work well if it were done by all of us. Consider not the individual consumer, but the whole body. What would help if *all* consumers followed a given course? This is the test; not what would happen if any one person acted in a given way, but if a very great many persons acted in that way.

Let us apply this obvious test to one proposal that is often made. The consumer of late has been much urged to spend to the limit at once. He has been told to buy now, and to buy all he can; to buy a house, stocks and bonds, clothes, playthings for the children—anything in sight. It matters little how you spend. Put in circulation all the money you can. Speed up the pace of buying all around.

I believe this is bad advice. A sudden burst of all-around spending is not the remedy for the present distresses. It means that a pace is taken which cannot be kept up. It means a spurt, and then a halt. If everyone does this, more goods are suddenly sold than before, dealers replace their stocks, producers turn out what *seems* to be wanted—and then the thing drops. People cannot buy continuously in this way; and it is continuity, a settled and steady movement of goods from producer to consumer, that brings the needed readjustment. The more the action is hurried, the more it is pumped up and unspontaneous, the less it is deliberate and discriminating—the worse are the after effects. It is precisely the fevered and excessive buying of the boom period, often pumped up by advertising and by instalment payments, that was among the causes of the collapse and our present troubles. That also meant a pace by consumers which could not be kept up. A grand orgy of expenditure is a dangerous stimulant, likely to be followed by a relapse. This course leads not toward readjustment, but toward more maladjustment.

But the extreme opposite is no better. The consumer is sometimes advised to refrain from spending —to practice more thrift, forethought, caution. True, you should live within your income, and should be very careful about mortgaging your future income. But do not suddenly hoard or stint. It is as bad to slow up suddenly as to speed up suddenly. That, also, is spasmodic, discontinuous, deranging. It is like putting on the brakes abruptly and stopping the car with a jolt. And, if we all go to the extreme of actually hoarding—if we all put cash in a stocking or a safe-deposit box—we withdraw just that much from the channels of monetary circulation, and still further derange the whole economic mechanism.

In the main, then, the consumer should follow the even tenor of his way. Let him buy what he needs, what he wants, what he can pay for. At this present time, the consumers are confused, blocked, hesitating. Many of them, indeed, as we know too well, have to face reduced incomes; not a few have no incomes at all. But it must be remembered that, while there are large numbers who have less to spend than two years ago, or even nothing to spend, the work of the world does go on. The great majority are still consumers and buyers. Let them turn their purchases to the things which are of continuing interest and value to them. The producers will then see what it is possible to put on the market regularly and continuously, and what they can sell at a decently paying price, not for a month only, but year in and year out.

This process will gradually work out toward normal conditions. We see here and there, in every part of the country, some industries and concerns that are doing well. People buy the products of these industries at paying prices. Sometimes the articles are new; sometimes they are familiar things dressed up in new guise; often just the good old things that one does not tire of. A drift of this kind can be seen—I mention possibilities at random—with new cotton goods, attractive and not expensive; new foods that help to vary our diet; household equipment that makes the housewife's day easier; automatic heating apparatus, electric devices, and so on. Here we see the process of readjustment. It takes time. But the repeated choices and responses work out their effects, and industry takes a direction and a pace that it can maintain. It is the silent, sober, well-weighed expenditure by thousands, hundreds of thousands, millions of individuals and households that will help to bring order out of confusion. Meanwhile, at the other end, business is feeling its way. Thousands and thousands of concerns are watching their sales, and trying to make out what is in demand at prices that will pay. It is their watchful response to steady demand that will cause production to flow in the right channels.

This, to repeat, is a slow process. It is made the

more slow in our present depression by the other factors which I have already mentioned: the psychological effect of long depression; the bank failures and financial disorganization; the international entanglements. These are matters on which something can be done at once; something actually accomplished in short order, by Congress—by passing a law. Among them, to mention just one, I am convinced that a helpful step would be to cut out the whole business of war reparations and interallied debts. But no single step is a panacea. There is no panacea. Least of all is there any panacea for bringing about the right proportionment of production to consumption. There is no quick-acting medicine for that adaptation. It must come gradually. The producer must adjust himself to the wants of the consumer; and the consumer should refrain from giving false leads to the producer.

Let me make a comparison, between the doctors and the economists. When a physician has a patient who has had a bad shock, and a serious illness thereafter, and is beginning to settle down to the fact that he has been ill and still is ill, the physician tells the sufferer to have a care. Keep quiet, and expect no quick and sudden recovery. Make no false starts; try no rapid-cure medicines. Nature has a way of bringing convalescence in ways that we doctors don't quite understand but which we see in operation again and again. When we have used what remedies there are for palliating and tiding over a severe attack, the best we can do is to let nature take her course. The doctor will say to his patient, You are all right at bottom and will get well— but be in no hurry, try to resume your normal routine as you find yourself able, and avoid stimulants and overexertion; and in time you will be yourself again.

Something of this sort we can say about industrial calamity and industrial recovery. Communities do recover from them, as individuals do recover from illness. Somehow the economic body knits itself together again, as the physical body does. We cannot discern just how it happens; the process is obscure; but happen it does. Keep quiet, and you will find a gradual readjustment to settled industrial conditions. Expect no spectacular turn; await slow betterment. Meanwhile live simply and normally, buy what you need, do not squander your spending power and do not stint. Something like nature's processes in the physical body takes place in the industrial body—a multitude of inconspicuous and invisible steps, all combining to bring about health once more.

In every great emergency, whether of war or peace, most people wish to do their bit. In the present depression, many, many men and even more women have been thus stirred. They have turned to the business friends whom they value, to public officials, and to economists, asking what they can do. How can they help; and help not merely by contributing directly to the needy, but by so regulating their daily lives as to promote recovery? Our answer is simple. Keep as much as you can to the even tenor of your way. Do not spend recklessly, do not be stingy. Do not waste, do not hoard. Help your neighbor, help your community, help your country, by making all the contributions you can for alleviating distress. Your gifts for charity and for public use will help, even though they are palliatives, not remedies. Things that bring some relief from pain and misery are as much needed in industry as they are in medicine. In your daily life, avoid excesses; live your own sober, steady, normal life. By so doing, you help to steady business life and help to bring it into the course of enduring health and prosperity.

RESPONSIBILITY AND ECONOMIC DISTRESS

Rexford G. Tugwell

THREE years ago we Americans were congratulating ourselves on what was apparently the best economic system ever devised. It seemed clear that we had discovered the secret of permanent prosperity. Those years seem to us now to have been a kind of Golden Age. The busy factories, the loaded trains, the crowded highways everywhere gave evidence. Most of us had jobs and homes and plenty to eat and wear. Now millions of us are jobless and uncounted numbers are homeless and hungry. The once busy factories are idle; the trains run half-empty; the highways are not so crowded. An old disaster has come upon us—the evil magic of depression.

Only here and there is there agreement among the experts concerning the causes of this sudden terrifying change. One of these is that the weeds of depression were sprouting in the very soil of that prosperity we had thought permanently devoted to useful plants. Those busy factories were preparing idleness for men and machines. The goods they made were passing out into the channels of trade loaded with so heavy a weight of prices that consumers could possess them only by being helped with a sudden expansion of installment selling. This was all right for the time being, but a day of reckoning came, the stimulants failed, and the dead hand of depression was suddenly laid upon all the land.

Was this the fault of business men? It would be foolish to blame a hard-working group of people, each of whom had done his daily task as he had been taught to do it, who had played the game of profit-making according to the accepted rules. Besides, business men have suffered along with all of us; they cannot knowingly have been blind to their own interests. The truth is that the fault is neither that of business men, nor of consumers, nor of the government, nor of anyone else. The fault lies in the rules by which the game of business is played. But who makes the rules? Well, all of us do; or rather we do not. For the difficulty is that we are trying to operate a new, integrated industrial system according to old, "let-alone" political ideas. And they do not fit each other.

The very fact that we can find no one to blame ought to tell us all we need to know by way of criticism. What comes after that is to discover what kind of new institutions we need; and then to discover what changes are required in our present system. Order and regularity in production and consumption, security of jobs and income, are all possible to us. It is merely a question of keeping those factories running and those railway trains moving. But this is what we have never been able to do because it was no one's responsibility. Each of us has done our little bit; but the big job of fitting everything together has gone by default.

We have assumed that impulses being conceived here and there will lead a great variety of people to undertake all necessary tasks because if they do they can earn a profit. We have held out profit as the ultimate reward. Industrial tasks undertaken in this way are reminiscent of nature's generosity with the seeds of her plants. She scatters millions that one may grow. And we allow a similar waste in business enterprise. Ninety-nine out of a hundred enterprises come to an early end, bringing not only disappointment but a waste of resources. We heap riches upon the one in a hundred which does grow. These profits may be used as the owner of the enterprise sees fit. We make no attempt at control or direction. What each has gained is his to do with as he likes. The difficulty with this is that what he likes to do is to use his gains in such a way as to produce more profit, and this may lead to trouble. For there is as much waste here as there is in allowing, as we do, the free undertaking of enterprise. The greater number of little businesses die before they grow big; and a certain amount of the profit we allow the larger ones is used in ways which are undesirable. Each of us uses his gains to further his own affairs; but in doing this we involve ourselves in such general troubles as face us now. Our system is one which fails to identify the interests of each with the interests of all.

Profits used to expand operations have given us in the United States a plant which almost never operates at full capacity. This, of course, raises costs; prices have to be higher; and consumers' incomes are simply not great enough to buy the resulting goods. Waste of this kind, as well as the waste of starting enterprises which fail, must be paid for. We pay for it in the prices of our goods; and when prices are so high that consumers cannot buy, the goods pile up in warehouses until factories are forced to close. Unemployment follows, and loss of wages, and then still fewer people can buy.

All this is no one's fault. It results from the way things are organized. We ought not to be surprised if we get what we have prepared for. The problem we have before us is to devise a set of institutions which provide for order and regularity rather than waste and periodic failure. The problem seems especially acute in times of widespread distress, such as the present. But in reality it is not one which can be settled by emergency measures, but only by careful efforts of revision and planning. We have to start by admitting that there is only one agency whose scope is wide enough to cover all businesses and all interests, which represents all of us, and to which we can safely intrust the necessary power: this is the federal government. Many industries are bigger than our states; this makes state control impossible. Industry itself cannot be trusted with power because industry necessarily looks at the consuming public as a market for its goods. Its prices for them will always be dictated by a drive for profits rather than by a desire to have goods and services used as widely as possible.

We are faced with the necessity of revising our laws—including the Constitution—so that the federal government may assume those powers and duties which must belong to it if we are to escape the present dilemma. These are the reasons for the widespread current interest in economic planning. To plan means to forecast the needs of consumers for goods rather than the need of business men for profits; and it involves setting out seriously to arrange that these needs shall be met. The requirements of such a scheme are drastic but they seem drastic only because they have been too long delayed. The invention of scientific management, and the turning over to machinery of more and more work which was once clumsily done by men, has revolutionized the relations between production and consumption. We have a productive system capable of literally flooding the country with goods if its powers could be released. This fact of greater capacity, and the contrasting fact that consumers cannot buy as many goods as can be produced, have for a long time been preparing difficulties. And all the time this has been happening we have done nothing to bring about the political changes which would enable consumers to buy what they must buy to keep our system going. The penalty of our delay is upon us, and, if the steps we must now take seem drastic, it is still urgent that we should take them.

We have an old notion that that government is best which governs least, which was fostered by a long fight for individual liberty. By a species of false reasoning we have transferred this fear that we may lose our liberties to another field and have held it to mean that there must be no governmental control of business. "To keep the government out of business" may be an aim which pleases the speculative and romantic reactionaries among business men, but the more enlightened of them have seen that it is just this attitude which makes regularity impossible, and that regularity is necessary if we are to avoid depressions. The further truth, which not many are as yet willing to admit, is that control by even more highly organized monopolies than those we have now is not enough; that this does not change the profit-making purpose of business; and that organizations devoted wholly to profit-making will always be under compulsion to exploit consumers.

The federal government is the natural repository of that power which can bring order into industrial affairs. To lodge it there it will first be necessary that the public shall want it and press for it. That both President Coolidge and President Hoover have rejected this idea shows how strong the opposition is and how far we are from accepting the logic of present necessity. It is strange that two successive chief executives should have volunteered themselves as critics of the government of which they were heads, and should have expressed disbelief in the ability of the government to carry this burden.

They reflect an attitude from which we must escape unless we are willing to have affairs managed exactly as they have been, or perhaps worse, as industrial power concentrates and grows stronger.

Business men themselves are willing to go part way in reorganization. They would like to see those laws revised which prevent combinations. By joining within their own industries they can take the first steps toward planning. But they usually reject the suggestion of federal control over the organizations they would like to build up. In this they are supported by a public opinion which has a profound distrust of government—perhaps justified up to now. It must be remembered, however, that we have never yet intrusted really vital functions of this kind to our federal government and that it might perform quite differently if it had so vital a task of supervision.

It is rather remarkable that there is scarcely a critic of the only body of this sort we have so far set up—the Interstate Commerce Commission. And we have no good reason to suppose that other similar economic controls would work less well. What we are likely to achieve soon, perhaps, is merely an "advisory" body for planning. There is now pending in Congress a bill to establish such a body. But this can be only a first step. Advice will not be enough. And sometime we shall turn to outright control, for only in that way can we tie the profit-making purpose of business to the uses of public service.

(135)

Speakers who will follow on successive Saturday nights will explore these matters further. They will consider the idea of planning as it is now used elsewhere in the world and as it might be applied in the United States. If you will follow their reasoning you will find yourself introduced to the general scheme of reorganization which many of us believe is the single best way to avoid economic distress in the future.

THE IDEA OF PLANNING

George Henry Soule, Jr.

M Y GREAT-GRANDFATHER'S farm in the state of Maine never was bothered by unemployment or overproduction. There were industrial depressions even in that day, but the farm knew little of their effects.

The family usually had plenty to eat, enough to wear, and leisure enough to have a good time. The folks did have to contend with natural enemies like drought, marauding animals, and disease, but not with confusion in their own work. They raised almost everything they needed to eat. They arranged the sowing, cultivation, and harvesting of crops and the culture of domestic animals so that each would do his share, and there would be enough product for all. The grain was ground into flour for the family at the local grist mill. The necessary timber was cut off the place and sawed at the saw mill. Skins were tanned for leather, and the leather was made into shoes by the local or the itinerant shoemaker. Some spinning and weaving was done by the women of the family, and simple clothing was sewed by them. The other garments were made by the tailor who traveled about. The family traded in its small surplus produce for the few things it had to buy, like

(137)

sugar and tea. Money played a very small part in satisfying its needs.

This farm family practiced a planned economy on a small scale. Its activities were laid out carefully in advance, so that duties would be performed at the right season, and there would be enough laid by for winter. The crops planted were adjusted to the needs both for food and for sustaining the farm animals. There never was any fear of a surfeit of goods —how could there be? The better the family coöperated in doing its work, and the more intelligently it regulated its activities, the more every member of the family had to eat and wear. And, of course, the head of the family would have thought it crazy to overdo any one branch of production at the expense of the rest. If he found himself in the middle of winter with hundreds of pounds of honey but no meat, he would have nobody but himself to blame. Only an idiot would get into such a position.

But idiotic difficulties of this sort are apparent in the affairs of our great national family today—indeed, in the whole world-family. We say that we have produced too much wheat, coal, and oil, although at the same time there are millions of people who haven't enough to eat or enough fuel with which to keep themselves warm. The farmers who have more wheat than they can possibly use cannot exchange the wheat for the manufactured goods which they require. The unemployed in the cities have an enormous amount of labor to offer to anyone who would buy it, but there is nobody to hire them. At the same time, the great industries have acres of plant and machinery which are lying idle, because the unemployed and the farmers cannot buy what these things might be producing.

What is the reason for this strange state of affairs? There are many intricate theories to account for it, but the broad fact about the existing chaos is quite simple: our modern system of production and distribution has not been planned with the same degree of common sense that was used in planning the old self-sustaining farm. If my great-grandfather could be brought back, and could be shown how we conduct our affairs, I do not think he would take long to put his finger on the sore spot. He would conclude that we had been acting like a lot of wild Indians, because, as a nation, we had gone ahead without any foresight or calculation as to just what we wanted to accomplish, and how we were going to do it.

Nowadays, he would see at once, each family does not and cannot produce everything it needs, and consume everything it produces. Nor does each factory, or city, or state. Economically we are all one big family, each member of which has to do his part in production, and each member of which has to use the products of many others. There is no help for that—modern machinery and railroads have specialized our duties and widened our areas of interchange beyond hope of turning back to the old self-sustaining farm community. But we have not acted co-operatively as one big family to produce exactly as much of each one thing as we wanted to consume and to see that each consumer got what he needed in exchange for the work he did.

As a people, we have had no production plan, and no consumption plan. We have devoted money and labor to making plants and machinery, to erecting buildings, and to developing land, faster than we have distributed money to the persons who were supposed to buy the products of this equipment. We have allowed some prices to get so high in relation to other prices that the products in question cannot be exchanged. As a result, the whole business is in confusion.

In spite of the fact that we can produce a great many more goods with less effort than could my great-grandfather, many of us are much poorer and less secure than he was. This is because each factory and each farm has gone about its work without sufficient relation to what others were doing. Some of our leaders dignify this confusion with the phrase "rugged individualism." Lack of gumption, he would have called it. If his family had gone at their work under such a hit-or-miss system, and if his boys and girls had justified the fact that everything was at sixes and sevens because they arranged their jobs, not in co-operation and under a far-sighted plan, but in response to the uninstructed dictates of their several rugged individualities, he would have told them to stop their nonsense.

Economic planning is often described as if it were

something wholly new and strange, as something which could not be practiced without changing human nature. I think the idea of planning is as old as civilization itself, and that the impulse to use foresight in organizing one's job and one's group is one of the most fundamental traits in human nature. What is new is not the idea of planning or the habit of organizing work, but the application of this idea and this habit to areas as broad as whole industries or whole nations. We are just waking up to the fact that the machine, the railroad, and all the other modern inventions which we have accepted have knit all the citizens together so closely that we cannot act any more as if planning could stop with the work of separate individuals or separate farms or separate factories. If each of us goes on serving his own interest without thought of the others, we are all bound to end in a jam.

Even the idea of planning for industries or for a whole nation is not wholly foreign to us. Industrial engineering has developed management on the basis of science in recent years. Frederick W. Taylor, an ingenious American, many years ago, began to establish the science of management. He started with intelligent organization of the individual workplace in the factory. He watched the worker at his job to see whether he was doing it in the best possible way. Was the machine or the tool as well adapted to its use as possible? Were the materials right? Did the worker go through any waste motions? Accurate research discovered better methods of work. It established standards of production. It fixed responsibility for output. The old way had been to follow habitual methods of work and depend for results on driving the worker with the traditional discipline of rewards and punishments. The new way was to find out the best way of doing things and set up standards and a definite program of work which depended on these standards. Then the co-operation of everyone concerned had to be enlisted to see that these standards were carried out. In this way, each man's output was greatly increased.

But this sort of thing could not stop with the individual work-place. The work-places had to be co-ordinated with one another. The flow of partly finished goods through the factory had to be regulated so that there would be neither stoppages nor gluts. Separate departments had to be combined into a harmonious whole. So the followers of Taylor went on to larger units, until they learned how to co-ordinate the activities of gigantic concerns having many plants. But always the science of management used the same principle and the same methods. The first necessity was research, to discover the facts of the situation and to set up the best procedure. The next was to record this procedure, and the results required, as a set of standards and a definite program. The next was to see that everyone co-operated in carrying out this procedure and these standards and in achieving this program.

Now the more intelligent experts in management are saying that it is not enough to carry out this precise organization even for single great industrial concerns. For the plans of these concerns are often knocked sky high by the uncertainties and accidents which occur outside them. We still leave to habit, to chance, to planless competition, the relationship among companies and among industries. This produces confusion which makes it difficult to obtain regular and efficient operation in the smaller units. So, in one sense, national planning is just an extension of the best American engineering practice.

Another important source of our ideas on this question was the national economic planning which the United States did during the World War. We had to take about one-quarter of our man power out of their usual occupations and put them either into the army and navy or into jobs supplying the army and navy with all the weapons and facilities of destruction. We had to supply a large part of the armies and populations of the associated powers. We had to transport troops and supplies across an ocean infested with submarines which limited the available ships, and, at the same time, we had to sustain the civilian population as usual. If we had relied on our ordinary confused economic arrangements to do this job, we should have failed miserably. But, of course, we could not, and did not.

We worked out schedules showing what was needed by the army and navy, by the Allies, by our domestic population. Those schedules revealed what it was most important to produce, and in what order the requirements had to be met. We organized our own industry to produce what was required and to do so in the proper order. We took over the railroads and shipping in order to make sure that transportation facilities would be used as efficiently as possible. We regulated fuel to see that it should go to the places where it was most needed, not just to the buyers who could pay the most for it. We regulated the food industries to make sure that everyone should be fed, and that no one should have more food than he needed as long as food was lacking elsewhere. All this, done in a great hurry, involved a great deal of disorder and waste and annoyance, as well as some injustice. But the amazing fact is that while we devoted about one-quarter of our man power to destruction, at the same time we produced enough necessary and useful goods, and distributed them well enough, so that the whole population lived about as well as it ever had before.

If this could be achieved inside of eighteen months, by the use of research and planning on a national scale, it stands to reason that with more time, and by aiming to enhance the general well-being instead of to injure an enemy, by trying to increase the output and consumption of useful things instead of making shells and poison gases and guns and tanks and destroyers, we could greatly improve the welfare of our country. We could abolish slums and poverty and unemployment, carry out reforestation, make sure that everyone was engaged in really useful work for which he might receive an adequate recompense, and increase the time for leisure and recreation.

Of course, we should have to have the common will to achieve these results. We should have to have precisely defined aims which could be set up as a guide to the control of production and consumption. And we should have to be ready to co-operate for the common ends. But the war proved that, given these things, we have the intelligence and the resources to plan nationally. The methods and instruments of peace-time planning would necessarily differ from those of war-time planning, but the important thing to remember is that we have in this country successfully employed planning on a national scale.

A great deal of the recent interest in planning has been derived from the experience of Soviet Russia, which is the first nation ever to practice thorough-going national planning for peace-time purposes. This experience will be discussed in a future talk in this series. It seems to me that we should not reject the idea of peace-time planning just because there is so much hostility in this country toward the Russian Revolution. That would be as silly as it would have been for our forefathers to discard democracy just because democracy in France was one of the achievements of the French Revolution. That upheaval, in its day, was hated and feared fully as much in the rest of the world as the Russian Revolution is now. We must remember that planning in the general interest has its roots in our soil just as it has in Russia, and that industrial civilization all over the world has reached the beginning of an era where great and historic changes must be made. All nations will probably not follow the same course in making these changes. But if we can learn anything to our own benefit by checking up on the Russian experience, by all means let us do so.

The chaos in which the world now labors should lead us to investigate carefully the various projects for planning. Succeeding talks in this series will deal with more detailed aspects of a problem which we can no longer safely evade.

PLANNING IN WESTERN EUROPE

Lewis L. Lorwin

THERE is an oriental proverb that the Lord provides the remedy before he sends the disease. This thought cheers many today in the midst of misery and chaos. They feel that before the present world-crisis gave the impetus, the imagination of man had already leaped in advance of the facts and reached out for a new idea with which to vanquish the enemy that was approaching. That idea is economic and social planning.

To most Americans, economic planning is a Bolshevik invention exemplified in the Five-Year Plan. As a matter of fact, the Russian Bolshevists are not the originators of economic planning. Its seeds were planted before the World War. During the war, it was the United States government which applied the principle on a large scale through the War Industries Board, the War Trade Board, and other federal agencies. And it was in Germany that the theory of a planned economy was worked out more fully between 1917 and 1919 under the pressure of the needs of post-war reconstruction.

In this respect, planning is having the same experience as other great and new social ideas. In the case of democracy, it was English philosophers and

American colonists who prepared the way, so that France could proclaim to the world the philosophy of democracy in the Declaration of the Rights of Man. And within the last twenty-five years American engineers and social reformers the world over have hammered out the methods of technical control now being used by Russia in developing the Five-Year Plan, which exemplifies to the world the idea of economic and social planning in the most spectacular manner.

Because human progress has mysterious and devious ways, the masses of the people have often stumbled in their grasp after truth and salvation. The path of democracy was obstructed by the fright and fury of the French Revolution. And now the newer ideas and principles of planning are enveloped in passions and prejudices aroused by the fear that the dictatorial and revolutionary planning of Russia is the only kind possible.

But as democracy in the nineteenth century became an idea, not of any one country but of all countries, and was modified to suit the needs of each country, so is planning destined to become a world-idea and to be adapted to the changing needs of each nation. Every day we see more clearly how all of us have helped to build up the idea in the past and how much of it we have already realized under existing conditions. And every day, as our economic individualism and laissez faire lose ground, we have an ever widening area of economic and social life where we are impelled to plan ahead, to apply the methods of science, and to exercise the conscious control of the community for common ends.

It is true that Soviet Russia has the only complete system of economic planning in existence today. Hers is by far the biggest single job of central control and management in human history, and there is little doubt that planning is making Soviet Russia into an industrial power, laying the foundations for a higher standard of living and for a new mode of social life.

The Western World refuses to accept the Soviet type of planning for reasons which seem valid enough. Soviet planning is combined with principles of property and methods of government which seem to many too harsh, too undemocratic, and too injurious to the individual. And it involves a violent break with the present which few are prepared to make and which many wish to avoid.

If economic planning could be of one type only, namely, the Soviet type, we would either have to accept it with all its features or reject it altogether. However, we do not face such a dilemma. The essence of planning is the conscious use of all available productive resources to give all the people the highest possible standard of living. With this end in view, the methods of planning can be applied in several ways and can be combined with different political and social institutions.

This is illustrated by the story of planning in Western Europe which, though partial in scope, is many sided in form. Take, for instance, Germany.

More than any other Western country, Germany illustrates the attempt to apply economic planning in a democratic way. What Germany has been doing has been to limit more and more the scope of unrestricted individualism or laissez faire by means of government control, of government-operated enterprises, and of special forms of industrial self-government. The direct operation of economic enterprises by the state has been developed to a very high degree, including the post-office, telephone, telegraph, railways, street-car lines, utilities, mining, manufacturing, and banking. While these enterprises are a form of state capitalism, the coal, iron, and potash industries represent examples of controlled industrial self-management. Each one of these industries has a central council composed of delegates from workers, employers, and consumers whose task it is to set conditions of work, to regulate prices, and to exercise general direction with regard to the interests of the country, subject to the supervision and control of the Ministry for Economic Affairs. The purpose of it all is to overcome the unforeseen workings of unregulated economic forces and to plan prices, wages, opportunities, and obligations in a way which may be best for the nation as a whole.

All these schemes are partial applications of the idea of planning. But Germany also has a National Economic Council, which is provided for in the German Constitution and which is an entirely new institution in the history of the world. It consists of several hundred delegates, representing the organized economic elements of the country—farmers, manufacturers, merchants, bankers, workers, artisans, and so on. Besides helping the government and parliament in shaping immediate economic and social legislation, this Council is thinking of German economy as a whole, and is studying long-range policies which may help to give German social life new direction and steadiness.

Compared with Germany, France has fewer elements of planning in her economic and social life, and the industrial activities of the French government are not so large. But, in some ways, France during the last forty years has planned even more effectively than other countries, namely, to maintain a balance between the various parts of her economy. That has been done largely through her tariff policy, which encouraged domestic agriculture as a basis for relative economic self-sufficiency.

For the past seven years France has also had a National Economic Council, which embodies in a large way the idea of co-operation toward common national ends. This Council has helped the government in planning the improvement of docks, harbors, railroads, shipping, etc., and is at present engaged in a survey of French industries for the purpose of preparing a new program for their rational reorganization.

Italy, as we all know, has been trying to combine planning with Fascism. When the Fascists came into power in 1922, they had no definite economic program. But being pragmatists and opportunists, they took up some of the proposals made before by other parties. Fascist efforts since 1925 have centered on the development of hydraulic power for industrial uses, on the electrification of the state railroad system, on the intensification of wheat production, and on furthering reclamation. It is in this latter field that the Fascists can claim their greatest successes. The so-called Mussolini Act, passed in 1928, has given additional impetus to the movement which has for its purpose the reclamation of over nine million acres of land. Through this reclamation scheme, the Italian government is hoping to change the flow of population, to keep the people from going to the cities or to foreign countries, and to develop a new agricultural population.

Italy has also been developing a new economic structure which may serve as a foundation for a national planned economy. Syndicates and corporations bring workers and employers together for the promotion of industry, and at the top is a Council of Corporations which supervises and controls their work. These are the basis of the "corporate state" which is built on the philosophy that the national good is the supreme value, that production is a public function, which may be intrusted to private individuals only as long as they perform it well, and that class conflicts must give way to co-operation between all groups for the general interest. On the basis of this philosophy, the Fascist government regulates prices, orders reductions in wages and

profits, or forces a reorganization of the entire banking system of the country when, in its opinion, conditions demand such action. And, though the Fascist
government hesitates to take the full step which its
philosophy would warrant, it is more and more
driven in the direction of control and planning by
events and by the logic of its own being.

Partial examples of planning can also be found in
Western Europe outside of Germany, France, and
Italy. In Great Britain, Czechoslovakia, Yugosla-
via, Spain, and several other countries, there are
national economic councils which are intrusted with
the task of studying the possibilities of co-ordinating national economic life. In Great Britain, especially, the idea of planning has made much progress
recently, and a number of private committees are at
work upon various phases of British life with the
idea of preparing a comprehensive national plan
within the next two or three years.

But, you may ask, what is the value of all this? Is
not Germany on the verge of economic collapse? Is
not Fascism a denial of democracy? Are not all the
countries of Western Europe in a state of distress?
Of what use has planning been to them so far, and
what can it do in the future?

The answer is that planning would have to be applied on a much larger scale than it has been to pull
Western Europe out of the mess in which it was left
by the World War. But even the small dose of planning in Western Europe has been effective. A great
deal of the stability which Western Europe has

shown since 1919 has been due to the partial planning which has been applied to maintain a more reasonable distribution of goods through wage and
price controls and through social insurance. If most
countries of Western Europe have been able so far to
steer a middle course between extreme dictatorships
and violent revolution, it has been largely because
they have used conscious effort to modify the hap-
hazard workings of laissez faire. We have the most
dramatic example of this today in Germany where
Chancellor Bruening is trying to apply planful methods on a basis of private property in the desperate
struggle to keep Germany from going to extremes.

From the experience of Western Europe with economic and social planning, one may draw three
main conclusions. In the first place, it shows that,
to make planning peaceful and democratic, the special groups which hold a privileged position in
society today must make real concessions to the
needs of the people and make industry serve large
social ends. Second, it shows that the partial application of planning in a few industries or in a few
governmental enterprises is inadequate for the solution of the great problems which vex us. The paradox of want and misery amidst growing productive
resources, which mocks and challenges us today,
calls for a decisive and concerted attack upon the
central problem of raising standards of living. For
that, we must take a decisive step toward a more
complete system of planning, applied whole-heart-
edly, scientifically, and on a big scale. And, third,

it shows that Western Europe and America must make a big effort and pull hard together for a larger world-plan if all countries—east and west—are to have a new chance to work and to grow in freedom and peace.

PLANNING IN RUSSIA

Colston E. Warne

RUSSIA is a socialistic country of 160,000,000 people. It is a land of innovations—of stupendous changes in agriculture, industry, and human relations. Economic planning is but one of these innovations. It is consequently impossible to disentangle Russian planning from the socialistic system with which it is associated. Nor is it possible to measure the results which flow from economic planning alone.

The ownership of land, of transportation facilities, of banks, and of all important industry is in the hands of the government, which is in turn ruled by the Communist Party. Factories are organized into a close-knit system of some eighty state-owned concerns. In a given area each concern has complete control over production in its branch of industry. Vigorous trade unions cover all industry. The majority of the agricultural populace are now engaged in collective farming. Peasants pool their holdings under government guidance to the end that highly mechanized large-scale farming be substituted for the age-old methods. The government itself operates giant farms. Retail distribution is largely in the hands of co-operative stores owned by consumers, though some government stores exist. Private trade, private manufacture, and private farming are a vanishing carry-over from the old order.

The money system operates much as our own. Prices of all important commodities are, however, governmentally fixed. In the main, all income—save on government bonds—is the result of work. A propertied class is not tolerated. Wages are not, however, equal. Skilled workers are more highly paid than unskilled. More important to the success of planning than any of these items, however, is the existence in Russia of a considerable body of militant young workers—mostly Communists—with a zeal for making Russia the foremost country of the world despite its heavy burden of illiteracy, bureaucracy, and Asiatic traditions.

As employed in Russia, economic planning involves the operation of a State Planning Commission, a central governmental bureau, which through numerous subordinate and co-operating bodies prepares annual tasks for every field of production and for every educational and social activity. These tasks, when ratified by the government, become specific assignments for the year. The annual plans are, in turn, expected to fit into the pattern of broad estimates prepared to cover five-year intervals. The first of these five-year plans the Russians hope to complete this year.

In constructing in 1928 the first five-year blue print of national development, the man power, the natural resources, and the capital equipment were inventoried. It was decided to build up the heavy industries (iron, steel, coal), to expand transportation facilities, to start great projects of electrification, to train a large number of skilled workers, and to launch the mechanization and collectivization of agriculture. In all it was decided to lay the groundwork for a highly industrialized country.

The organization of the plan is too involved to be covered here. Suffice it to say that elaborate statistics are employed in the attempt to piece together the complicated pattern of agriculture, industry, construction, transportation, power, finance, trade, and the labor supply, in addition to fitting educational and cultural pursuits into the general picture. Specifically, in budgeting the output of an agricultural machinery factory, extensive conferences are held in which worker representatives, managers, and central planning agents seek to co-ordinate the program of that plant with steel, coal, transportation, agriculture, construction, and other fields. On January first of each year every industry—indeed, every factory—knows what it is expected to produce during the ensuing twelve months. Through periodic reports a check is kept on actual developments. Lagging industries are subject to immediate attention in order that the plan may not be imperiled by their failure.

The plan for 1932 was issued in mid-December. Somewhat gleefully the Russians announced to a depressed world their targets for the current year. Let me list a few of the more important ones: The national income of Russia is scheduled to increase

30 per cent; wages, 11 per cent; electrical power, 60 per cent; coal production, 50 per cent; steel production, 76 per cent. Eighty-two thousand tractors are to be made, a doubling of last year's output. A job is to be supplied to everyone, as in the past two years. Indeed, in the present year the plan is that three million additional workers not hitherto in wage work will be required—750,000 of whom are to be added to industrial pay-rolls. It is planned that public works and housing expenditures should be doubled. Railway tonnage should increase by 28 per cent. Expenditures of the central governmental agencies for cultural activities, including education, science, health, and social insurance are scheduled for an advance of 38 per cent. It is estimated that 56,000 will graduate from universities, 175,000 from technical schools, and 485,000 from factory schools.

This seems an ambitious program for one year. If achieved, the Russians will be able to state with confidence that their nation has advanced more rapidly in productive equipment and national income in four consecutive years than any country in the history of the modern world in a similar period. In these four years, they would have more than doubled their national income and capital. They would have increased the buying power of workers' wages by more than 60 per cent. They would have established the seven-hour day, as well as extensive social-insurance benefits. They would have substituted a new farming system for small-scale methods of tillage.

The Russians hold, however, that they have not yet hit their stride. With the completion of the present intense period of industrial construction and agricultural reorganization, a period marked by confusion and great sacrifices, they count on an even more rapid advance. Under the first plan they have been building their machine equipment. Under the second five-year plan, just announced, they expect not only to continue this construction but also to reap the rewards of sacrifice in tripling the amount of food, clothing, and other necessities that a Russian worker can buy with his wages. If the second five-year program keeps its charted course, the hours of labor will be reduced to six and production will far outstrip any European country. But this will not satisfy them. To quote Molotov, the chairman of the Council of People's Commissars: "The decade which we have entered is that decisive period in which we must not only overtake the capitalist countries . . . . but . . . . outdistance them."

Many, viewing these Russian pronouncements, will be reminded of the milkmaid in Aesop's fables who, when going to market with the pail of milk on her head, contemplated the money she would receive for the milk, with which she would buy fowls which would lay eggs which could be sold to the parson's wife, which money would buy a dimity frock and a chip hat which would make her the envy of her world. But, as you recall, the haughty toss of her head spilled the milk.

This skeptical view of Russian forecasts has but little justification in past experience. Though there has, indeed, been in Russia a tendency to count chickens before they are hatched, one must in fairness state that Russian production has for the nine consecutive years since the famine followed a persistent upward trend—a trend nothing less than spectacular. Annually for the past five years national income has risen above the level of the preceding year by 10 per cent, 12 per cent, 9½ per cent, 21 per cent, and 13 per cent, Soviet statistics indicate. Large-scale industry has shown even more striking gains. Even discounting these figures for a general lowering of quality, the increases have been most marked.

It is one thing to suggest that Russian production has rapidly been going forward and another to hold that it has followed the exact lines outlined in their planning. Indeed, one is tempted to wonder at times just which plan they are following. In 1926–27, a tentative five-year program was outlined. After two years of relatively successful operation, it was discarded in favor of a much more elaborate and ambitious five-year plan which had maximum and minimum variants for each year. Then, rendered enthusiastic by running beyond the maximum variant for the first year of its operation, drastic upward readjustments were made in the control figures for the second year. Production for that year failed to reach the new figures but was generally above the original targets. Last year, the estimates were again inflated with a consequent widening gap between expectations and results. Large-scale industry, for example, was slated in 1931 to better its record of the previous year by 46 per cent. Its actual rise was recorded as 26 per cent. The worst record was in the metals industry—especially in steel. Closer approaches to the planned output were made, however, in coal, oil, tractors, and shoes. This year the estimates seem as optimistic as ever.

To appraise Russian planning is difficult. One can, of course, easily suggest that it has failed to balance after the pattern of double-entry bookkeeping. Like any newly-created instrument, planning has been crude and inexact. It has suffered from the over-optimism of its sponsors. It has been deficient due to the speed with which the Russian economic system broke with traditional property rights, setting in motion almost unpredictable trends—such as the present overwhelming move of peasants from country to city. It has been inaccurate because of the varying performance of Russian managers and workers—the bulk of whom are new recruits to industry. It has been thrown out of balance because the unplanned outside world, overcome by depression, has accepted Russian exports at less than planned prices, thus forcing drastic curtailments of scheduled imports. The low quality of goods has been another serious problem. But, most of all, its difficulties have resulted from the inability of the planners to assemble adequate statistical material with the promptness demanded by the controls and to forecast and relate the trends in all fields of production. An economic plan is in many ways like a jig-saw puzzle—no piece may be misplaced without shifting the position of all other pieces.

There is, however, much to be said for economic planning in Russia. It has been the agency through which the limited national income of that country has been rapidly channeled into the creation of machine equipment for the hastening of industrialization. By saving a third of the national income today, it is hoped that bountiful supplies will be forthcoming tomorrow. Planning has also had a psychological value. The tempo of a slow-moving people has been quickened. In mechanics, in education—indeed, in the underlying culture—the drive of the five-year plan has been felt. Planning has become the symbol of an emerging socialist order. In a very real sense, the Russians have not wished precise planning—for such planning involves rather exact measurements of production with the certainty that exceeding the quotas would be as disastrous as failure to reach them. Rather the Russians have wished stimulus. And, by setting the planning estimates high and heralding the success of those workers who have exceeded them, they have secured an incentive.

In explaining the present tempo of Russian production, planning is not the most important item. The basic explanation must rather lie in the Communist Revolution which allowed a militant, class-conscious group to forge a socialist system in a land of immense, almost untapped resources. The land-owning nobility is gone. Parasitic classes have been driven out. In the place of a crude agriculture and a wasteful competitive industry controlled by a highly autocratic Tsarist government, socialism is securing a trial, under a rigid Communist control which embraces production, the press, and all educational channels—the "dictatorship of the proletariat" it is called in Russia. And socialism, even now, under these auspices, has shown immense productive superiority over their pre-war system, especially when one considers the comparative lack of foreign financial support given the new régime. The market is known and certain, with prices and purchasing power controlled by the government. Powerful human incentives have been discovered. Interfactory and interdepartmental rivalries for production have arisen. Small "shock brigades" of enthusiastic skilled workers have been rushed into lagging industries with wide popular acclaim. Resources have been quickly mobilized and shifted by the government. Above all, a spirit of experimentation and self-criticism has developed in the managerial group which has led to progress as well as to blundering.

To sum up: Russian economic planning has not as yet become a reliable guide. Planning has, however, acted as a powerful incentive to chart the course of Russia in the direction of rapid industrialization. Looking ahead, it is likely that planning will have an increasing place in Russian life. Through persistent propaganda an almost unbounded faith has been developed in a planned socialist order—a faith which holds that only through the Russian system may the machine be harnessed in the future to shorten the hours of labor, to advance living standards, to provide complete security against unemployment and old age, and to lay the basis for a deeper culture than that which characterizes the rest of the world. The Russians have come to feel themselves crusaders for a new and just cause. Indeed, it is their optimistic hope that their method of control and operation of industrial enterprise, as well as their social institutions, may soon become, not a Russian system, but a plan by which the idea of nationality may be subordinated to the establishment of a world economic order in which no propertied class exists, in which unemployment is a thing of the past, and in which personal ambition for wealth is replaced by a common concern for the social welfare.

The Russians feel that world-capitalism is breaking under the weight of insoluble problems. They hope that their system will prove so successful that its example will ultimately lead other nations into a world-union of socialist republics. We do not today have the evidence to assert whether or not the Russian ideas will prove superior. We do know that the production of Russia has increased rapidly and shows signs of continuing that increase. If, however, they do go forward at the pace they anticipate they will have to acquire a greater mastery over economic planning than they now possess.

BUSINESS PLANNING

Ralph C. Epstein

IT MAY seem queer for an economist to begin a talk on "Business Planning" by quoting poetry, yet this is what I should like to do. The most frequently heard figure of speech describing the industrial system is that which calls business a machine, but other less impersonal metaphors are possible. To the late William Vaughn Moody, modern business was less a machine than a monster, and of this potent but uncontrollable being he wrote in his poem "The Brute":

> Through his might men work their wills.
> They have boweled out the hills
> For food to keep him toiling in the cages they
>   have wrought;
> And they fling him, hour by hour,
> Limbs of men to give him power;
> Brains of men to give him cunning; and for dainties
>   to devour
> Children's souls, the little worth; hearts of wom-
>   en, cheaply bought:
> He takes them and he breaks them, but he gives
>   them scanty thought.
>
> For about the noisy land,
> Roaring, quivering 'neath his hand,
> His thoughts brood fierce and sullen or laugh in
>   lust of pride
> O'er the stubborn things that he
> Breaks to dust and brings to be.

> Some he mightily establishes, some flings down
> utterly. . . . .

"' 'Tis the Brute they chained to labor! He has
made the bright earth dim.
Store of wares and pelf a plenty, but they got no
no good of him.' "

We have, in other words, created an industrial
system with a colossal capacity for production, and
then lost control of the very set of devices which we
ourselves have created. How to achieve this control,
in the fullest desirable measure, is the problem of
business planning.

At the outset, it seems to me that any reasoned
consideration of economic planning needs to recognize two things. On the one hand, to retain complete individual freedom is unthinkable. To leave
each business alone to work out its own destiny is
today obviously an impossible policy even from the
point of view of the most conservative elements of
the community. On the other hand, a complete control of industry—in the sense of a detailed supervision of production and a continuous adjustment of
supply and demand in the case of all commodities,
undertaken by some central planning committee or
other regulatory body—is unrealizable and probably
equally undesirable.

What is required, therefore, is a compromise
policy which will preserve flexibility in production
and thus allow freedom in consumption. Yet such
a policy, while promoting the welfare of all members of the community as consumers, ought not to

oppress them as producers or imperil their solvency as investors. For in any free community, business planning, undertaken in the interests of the greatest number, must strike an intelligent compromise between a reactionary "let-alone" policy on the one hand and a restrictive, paternalistic one upon the other.

How can producers organize so as better to control the operations of each industry? *For organize they must; no one business unit can do anything alone.* Unless we condone business crises, unless we commit ourselves to constantly recurring industrial chaos, we have to recognize that the era of American individualism in large-scale enterprise is over. Business men simply must co-operate in making plans as to production, in frequently foregoing immediately realizable short-time profits for long-time stability, and in pooling knowledge and resources so as to insure their wage-earners steadier employment and a reasonable protection from the fear of involuntary idleness.

Granted a willingness on the part of the business men in any given industry to co-operate with each other, and granted the legal possibility of their being able to do so, three things become essential to the success of any scheme which aims to attain these ends. The first is the establishment of an adequate statistical bureau for the industry—a central headquarters to which members would currently report upon production, inventories, sales, and the like. I believe it absolutely essential, in this connection, that earnings and investment figures be reported as well. In spite of the fact that some businesses would be loath to report their profits, such figures are needed if a complete picture of economic trends, and of the increasing or shrinking opportunities for capital in any given industry, is to be had. Furthermore, if the community permits competing businesses thus to co-operate, through a partial relaxation of the Sherman Law, it is entitled to have such knowledge of earnings available as a public record.

The second requisite is frankness and honesty in the release of such statistical materials. It does no good to collect and tabulate sets of data, however excellent the technique of analysis, if, as Mr. Walter Gifford once said, we rose-tint their interpretation. We Americans need sorely to realize that optimism in itself is not a virtue; it is as much a vice as is unbridled pessimism. Both the newspapers and the trade journals of the country have much to answer for in this respect. Statistical data should be allowed to stand upon their own legs, so-called "unfavorable" items should never be suppressed—and I say this knowing full well what a strong word "never" is—and all reported information of whatever kind should be made available to the members of other industries and associations, and to the general public as well.

The third requisite is that the members of the industry really co-operate in the use of such pertinent information. Here the word "co-operate" loses its general character and is intended to have a very specific meaning indeed. In a few leading industries, as an experiment, we should at once give producers the legal power to plan—and this will sometimes mean to restrict as well as to expand—production. But they need not, and in my opinion should not, be given the power to merge plants, combine their outputs for selling purposes, pool profits, or agree upon prices.

The Sherman Law should be relaxed only so as to enable agreement as to the setting of intelligent production quotas, with reference to the actual and probable market demand for specific products. Business planning should not in the long run aim to curtail the total amount of goods produced. There is much popular misconception of the nature of overproduction; it is often alleged that more goods of all kinds are produced than can be used. But our difficulty is rather that some goods cannot be sold at a profit. Business planning should attempt to obtain for society a steadier and larger production of all goods by the careful and wise determination of the proper relative amounts of each *specific set of goods* to be placed upon the market at certain times and over certain periods.

The need and the possibilities for such co-operative action are seen in the experience of the automobile industry. In a recent address before the Academy of Political Science, I called attention to the spectacular circumstances of this case. In 1916, the motor industry passed its peak of growth, in terms of the yearly percentage of increase shown by its production curve. In 1922 or 1923, however, a "flattening out" of the actual figures began. This was clearly evident by 1926. Then was the time to have begun planning. But in that year, you recall, the competition of several producers of small cars began to encroach upon the sales of the Ford Company. The Ford Company therefore took a year off, in 1927, and changed its model. That gave General Motors and several other producers their big chance —they expanded output and sold thousands upon tens of thousands of cars while consumers could not get delivery of Model A Fords. Encouraged by their success in 1927, these companies greatly extended their plant capacities. The result was that in 1928 and 1929, with Ford back in production, the industry had more than enough capacity to take care of consumer demands even in those excessively prosperous years; and that, in any less active year, the industry is now saddled with capacity it cannot possibly use.

Now my point is this: If the producers of automobiles could have sat around a table in 1927 and said to each other, not figuratively but literally and legally, "See here, we know that we all can't expand our capacities and use them; the market isn't calling for anything like that many cars; let's tell each other our exact plans and then exercise a little restraint"—could that have been done not merely in the automobile industry but in several other important industries, a million fewer men might be out of work this winter.

Why should we not so experiment with a few selected industries which already possess well-organized trade associations and in which there are not so many small-scale producers as to make the experimental machinery too complicated or costly? I am aware that there are many difficulties involved in putting such a scheme for the co-operative allocation of extensions to plant capacity into actual practice. I am aware that the producers might not always agree as to the allocations among themselves, and that governmental supervision of the association might then be necessary. I am aware that, left to themselves, producers might even try to prevent desirable new enterprises from coming into their industry; and I am likewise aware that in the case of industries which manufacture staple products such as sugar or steel or copper, curtailing of production might sometimes be deliberately attempted in order to raise the price of the product. All that I have to say is that I grant any or all these things might happen; but do they present any consequences much worse than the situation which periodically now prevails under a system of free competition? If not, then I suggest that we undertake the experiment of co-operative planning, with all its hazards, in a few important directions, immediately.

But let me again emphasize that I am not recommending, as does Mr. Gerard Swope, that a large number of industries immediately organize to stabilize production and employment through conscious efforts. If all important industries and trades attempted to organize at once for such a purpose, the attendant confusion might be so great as to obliterate all chances for the plan's success. I suggest, rather, that *some three or four important industries* undertake both to experiment with a comprehensive scheme of unemployment insurance and to organize a board for the allocation of extensions to plant capacity over the course of the next business cycle. The government might well take the initiative in sponsoring the organization of such boards for those industries, and in acting as arbitrator or court of appeal if necessary. The experiment, being confined to but a few fields, could be carefully observed, and if the results were favorable, other industries could then follow with co-operative plans of their own.

In closing, I wish definitely to say that the scheme of co-operative "plant-extension-allocation" here suggested is not put forward as any industrial panacea. A depression such as the one through which we are now passing is the result of more things than merely unbalanced expansion in particular branches of manufacture. The stock market, the plight of agriculture, the gold problem and the international situation: those difficulties are being discussed by other speakers in this series on "Aspects of the Depression." But unplanned production and excessive plant capacity are at least important parts of our complicated problem.

We can only learn to control them through deliberate experiment, and I have no illusions that any rapid or complete success will attend such efforts.

But if we make a beginning in one or two directions, that in itself will make easier the struggle for mastery in other fields and over other parts of our problem. For it is, after all, fundamentally absurd that men have ingeniously created an industrial system for themselves and have then permitted it to rule them rather than force it to do their bidding. If we have the courage to experiment, is it too much to hope that some day, after years of conscious effort in which we prove ourselves a little less timid, a little less narrowly selfish, and a little less short-sighted than we are now, we may be able to say with William Vaughn Moody that the Brute:

[will] give each man his portion, each his pride and worthy place . . . .
On each vile mouth set purity, on each low forehead grace.

Then, perhaps, at the last day,
They will whistle him away,
Lay a hand upon his muzzle in the face of God, and say,
"Honor, Lord, the Thing we tamed!
Let him not be scourged or blamed.
Even through his wrath and fierceness was thy fierce, wroth world reclaimed!
Honor Thou thy servants' servant; let thy justice now be shown."
Then the Lord will heed their saying, and the Brute come to his own,
Twixt the Lion and the Eagle, by the armpost of the Throne.

FEDERAL PLANNING

Stacy May

ANY Russian school boy—at least, any Russian school boy who has studied his home work in Ilin's *New Russia's Primer*—knows what is wrong with the economic organization of the United States. For almost at the beginning of that sprightly and provocative book there is presented a comparison between the socialized economic organization of Soviet Russia and the competitive system of free private enterprise which is generally accepted as being so characteristically American.

> "We have a plan," Mr. Ilin chants.
> "In America they work without a plan.
>
> "We have a seeding campaign.
> In America they destroy crops.
>
> "We increase production.
> In America they reduce production and increase unemployment.
>
> "We make what is essential.
> In America hundreds of factories consume raw materials and energy in order to make what is entirely unnecessary."

This country, wisely or foolishly, as you wish, has not been notably cordial to suggestions from Soviet Russia, and if Mr. Ilin were alone in indicating our need for some sort of centralized economic control it is very improbable that a series of talks on economic planning would have been offered on this network. However, the genuinely desperate circumstances of industrial depression have created a new cordiality toward any plausible and honestly offered program for improving our economic arrangements. During the past year numerous recommendations have been made for the establishment of some form of organization, upon a national scale, for co-ordinating American business policies, with the view to mitigating the current depression or preventing its recurrence.

Perhaps the most noteworthy of these programs is that incorporated in "A Bill to Establish a National Economic Council" (S. 6215, 71st Congress, 3d Session) presented to the United States Senate by Senator LaFollette of Wisconsin. This bill provides for the appointment of a National Economic Council of fifteen members, to be selected from a list submitted by representative economic groups. The bill gives the Council broad powers for requiring business organizations to supply regular or special information, but it confers no power upon the Council for requiring co-operation with any program that it may evolve. It merely provides that the Council shall study general economic and business conditions and problems, shall make reports upon them, shall formulate economic policies, and shall recommend necessary legislation.

Early in 1931 the Senate adopted a resolution directing its Committee on Manufactures to make a study of this bill and of other proposals for economic planning, to conduct hearings on the subject, and to report back with its findings. The hearings were conducted by a subcommittee of the Senate Committee on Manufactures under the chairmanship of Senator LaFollette from October 22 to December 19, 1931. Some forty-five individuals testified, and expressed either approval or skepticism of the LaFollette Bill or of the general idea of economic planning. The provisions of a number of other plans were reviewed in the course of these hearings, three of which appear to have been singled out for special attention by the subcommittee.

One of these three programs was formulated by Mr. Gerard Swope, President of the General Electric Company, one by the Committee on Continuity of Business of the Chamber of Commerce of the United States, and a third by a subcommittee of the Committee on Unemployment and Industrial Stabilization of the National Progressive Conference. Since it is possible, in the time allotted, to make only the most general of references to the provisions of these three plans, it is earnestly recommended that those of you who are interested should review them at first hand. The complete hearings of the LaFollette Committee are readily obtainable through the Government Printing Office in Washington.

It is, of course, quite possible that the movement for the establishment of national economic planning will not proceed, in the near future, beyond the vocal stage. However, if it should, it is probable that the germs of any plan which may be attempted —whether through governmental or private initiative—will derive from the provisions of the LaFollette Bill and the three plans which have been named. It seems appropriate, then, to attempt some analysis of the similarities, the differences, and the general promise of these four proposals.

In the first place, it is noteworthy that all four of the plans provide for the gathering of statistical data and its interpretation by centralized authorities. Furthermore, all of the plans depend largely upon the development of voluntary co-operation on the part of private enterprise in carrying out any policies which may develop from such research. The Swope and the Chamber of Commerce plans would employ no compulsory machinery whatsoever for enforcing co-operation. The LaFollette Bill and the Progressive Conference program would seem to rely almost as much upon the voluntary co-operation of individual firms; but these last two plans contain provisions whereby the planning councils or boards may recommend legislation for the enforcement of their programs if such action becomes necessary.

Three questions arise, answers to which would appear to be necessary for any appraisal of the proposed measures for national planning. First, What need is there for new centralized agencies to gather, correlate, and interpret current economic statistics and to recommend economic policies? Second, What are the prospects, in our individualistic competitive system, of inducing private business concerns voluntarily to limit their production or sales policies in conformity with plans drawn to promote general social welfare? Third, What form would be taken by recommendations for legislation to enforce national economic policies, when voluntary co-operation was not forthcoming? These are all extremely complex and controversial problems. It is earnestly hoped that you will accept what is said about them as the humble opinions of one individual, expressed in such condensed form that they may well seem to reflect a dogmatism that is not intended.

First, then, there are numerous agencies gathering, publishing, and interpreting statistics about almost every conceivable detail of American economic life. Such work is done by trade associations, by many official agencies of the several states, and on an impressively large scale by various federal departments and governmental bureaus. In spite of the fact that there are serious gaps in our economic data —we have notably deficient information about unemployment and about inventories—it is not clear that such gaps cannot or will not be filled by existing agencies.

On the other hand, there is real reason to believe that interpretation of economic statistics has not kept abreast of their collection. If a national economic council were composed of men with sufficient insight and prestige, it is quite possible that it might perform valuable services. It would be in a position to make unified interpretations of data gathered by the many existing agencies and to command for such interpretations a much wider public hearing than existing agencies are able to achieve.

As to whether or not it is reasonable to hope that private business concerns will voluntarily adopt programs in conformity with a centralized plan, experience in this country would dictate a healthy skepticism. When Mr. Ilin, in the phrase from *New Russia's Primer*, says that American industry has no plan, he is correct only if that statement is to be interpreted as meaning that we have no one concerted plan for all industries, which would be comparable to the Five-Year Plan of Soviet Russia. But while we have not *a* plan, it is hardly exaggeration to say that the number of our *plans* is legion. Many of them, furthermore, are of national scope. The only difficulty is that there has been pitifully little success in getting private enterprise to conform to them. One or two conspicuous examples may be cited.

Since 1928, the Bureau of Agricultural Economics of the United States Department of Agriculture has issued annual reports on the "agricultural outlook." It attempts to help farmers make intelligent planting and breeding plans by supplying them with estimates of the probable market conditions at the time when their crops and animals will be ready for market. These reports are based on the best available information, domestic and foreign, on production, supply on hand, demand, and prices. Conferences are held at intervals to interpret this data upon a regional basis. Extension services in each state take the general figures and recommendations and recast them in such a form as to make them peculiarly relevant to the problems of each state.

The Bureau, in co-operation with state agricultural experiment stations, has made also elaborate studies of land resources, settlement, utilization, appraisal, value, and tenure. It has, as its avowed purpose, the development of a national policy for the most efficient land utilization.

In addition, the Federal Farm Board has aided in the promotion of systems of co-operative marketing agencies for most of the important agricultural products. It has attempted to control price and hence production in the fields of wheat, cotton, and butter. From a $500,000,000 fund it has made loans to co-operative associations and stabilization corporations. It has set up ten advisory commodity committees for developing plans for improvement of conditions in the fields of as many commodities.

It is difficult to visualize how any program for national economic planning which did not throw over free private enterprise and adopt compulsive tactics, could go farther in any one field than that which is now in existence for agriculture. And yet it would take a hardy, perhaps a foolhardy, enthusiast to claim for this elaborate program of national agricultural planning a conspicuous degree of success.

The difficulties are largely inherent in the system of free private enterprise. Few wheat farmers are ignorant of the fact that there is too much wheat to be marketed profitably. And yet if a few socially-minded growers plant less in a given year, while others plant as usual, the price is substantially unchanged, and the altruists find their incomes reduced while the interest on their mortgages and their taxes remain constant as the dawn. But if the millenium were to come, and a majority of wheat farmers were to cut their planting in two, it would then be highly profitable for individuals to diverge from the general program in order to have more wheat to dispose of at the profitable price level. It seems that enough are wont to succumb to such temptations to spoil the general programs.

If it be urged that farmers are notoriously individualistic, comparable difficulty may be cited in enlisting co-operation in industrial fields. The bituminous coal industry is admittedly in a chaotic condition. For years it has been limping along with a productive capacity of from 50 to over 100 per cent in excess of current demand. Unemployment is habitual, wages inadequate, profits sporadic, and losses chronic. The National Coal Association, the American Mining Congress, and the Council of American Mining Engineers have all devoted the most painstaking efforts to the task of diagnosing the industry's ills and planning remedies. Leaders of the industry agree that the stumbling block has been that no substantial co-operation has been achieved among the rival coal producers. Many have expressed the opinion that such co-operation is impossible of achievement upon a voluntary basis.

The cases cited may well fall under the head of horrible examples. But it would be difficult to find instances where voluntary conformity to general programs has been adhered to when individuals have found it profitable to digress. It is now urged that effective collaboration is prevented by the anti-trust laws, and hence their repeal or modification is advocated. But under current judicial interpretation it is perfectly legal for a trade association to gather and disseminate to its members complete information on the affairs of its industry. It may analyze this information in such a way as clearly to indicate policies which will promote general industrial welfare. It may not coerce its members to collaborate in promoting such policies. If the anti-trust laws were repealed it would be legal, presumably, to urge or require trade association members to enter into contracts binding themselves, for example, to adhere to given production quotas. But it is difficult to see why concerns which are unwilling to conform voluntarily to such policies, would voluntarily enter into such contracts. It would be easier to withdraw from the association.

Taken as a whole, then, the record of voluntary adherence to general programs on the part of American industrialists has not been inspiring, in peace times at least. It is difficult to see why one logically should expect more from it in the future.

We still have to consider the provisions of the LaFollette Bill and the Progressive Conference plan under which recommendations would be made for legislation to force recalcitrant individuals to conform to national policies. The LaFollette Bill is not specific here, but the Progressive Conference plan indicates that its National Economic Board might recommend that certain industries be declared to be public utilities and controlled as such, and that in others the government should itself enter into the conduct of the business. Both of these suggestions, obviously, if broadly exercised would constitute a very wide departure from the ordinary procedure of American business. Both of them promise to provide a degree of collaboration that hardly could be expected to materialize voluntarily. Each of them would raise a set of problems of its own which would demand solution.

Furthermore, it is far from clear, in view of recent decisions of the United States Supreme Court, that the list of industries declared to be public utilities may be extended indefinitely. And even where this form of control has been exercised most successfully —notably in the case of the Interstate Commerce Commission's control over railroads and the Federal Reserve's control over banking—there hardly has been conspicuous success in avoiding overexpansion or in attaining immunity from the evils of depression.

The whole criticism of programs for national planning may be reduced to this: Centralized planning and the exercise of individual initiative are fundamentally opposed. One can be promoted only at the expense of the other. The great difference between the economy of Soviet Russia and that of the United States is not that Russia has a centralized plan where we have none—it is that they have a highly centralized, socialistic system for carrying out a national plan, while we depend for our industrial adjustments primarily upon the individual decisions of private business executives. The men who direct private business must base their judgments upon the trend of markets as reflected in prices. When an attempt is made artificially to control prices, while judgments as to production and sales policy still are left in private hands, grave and cumulative errors necessarily are made. For, since governmental boards are not actuated by strictly commercial motives, their policies are not predictable in strictly market terms. In this way a *lit 'e* planning may be a very dangerous thing.

THE LIMITATIONS OF PLANNING

Sumner H. Slichter

NO ONE who contemplates the economic disaster in which we find ourselves today, or the plight of the numerous industries, such as coal, petroleum, or textiles, which were chronically "sick" even before the depression, can escape the conclusion that our ancient policy of "letting things take their course" is not working satisfactorily. The country is full of *individual* enterprises that are run well, but the industrial system *as a whole* evidently does not operate as it should. We have created the kind of economic system which cannot be trusted to run itself and, more or less against our will, we find ourselves compelled to experiment with methods of controlling industrial activities.

Already we have gone far in this direction, as is indicated by the work of the Interstate Commerce Commission, the Federal Reserve Board, the Federal Farm Board, and many other government bodies. During recent years the suggestion has frequently been made that we embark on a planned economy. Although the specific proposals vary greatly, one finds repeated again and again the two following general suggestions: first, that individual industries be permitted to organize themselves for the purpose of regulating competition and possibly controlling the investment of capital and the volume of output; and, second, that there be established a National Economic Council, or an economic general staff, composed of experts who, by collecting statistics on production, consumption, industrial capacity, and other factors, and by making recommendations in the field of economic policy, would seek to improve the operation of our industrial system.

It is usually suggested that the Economic Council should possess advisory powers only, with no authority to compel acceptance of its recommendations. Sometimes, however, it is suggested that the Council should possess some authority over the organizations established within particular industries, at least to the extent of requiring that adequate representation be given to all interests.

The ideal of an industrial system kept stable and free from depressions by the guidance of experts is attractive, but our experience with industrial control should prevent us from expecting too much. Not all "sick" industries are, like coal and textiles, uncontrolled. Railroading, one of the chief sufferers, is also among the most completely regulated industries. This does not mean that national planning is not worth attempting, but it does remind us that much of the planning in existence today is bad and that the successful control of industry will not simply *happen*—it must be *achieved*. In order to visualize clearly just what national planning of the voluntary sort could and could not accomplish, let us briefly examine: (1) the proposal to permit organizations within particular industries, and (2) the proposal to establish a National Economic Council with advisory powers.

No doubt organizations for the purpose of enabling each industry in some degree to regulate itself are becoming increasingly necessary. Regulation there must be, and yet the state legislatures and Congress are often too ill-informed and too burdened with other matters to provide it. But, although organization within industries is for many reasons becoming more urgent, it should be stated emphatically that such organization would not prevent slumps in business and might even aggravate and prolong them. It would not prevent them, because depressions are produced by causes of a very general nature, such as the mismanagement of the credit system and changes in the rate at which capital is invested. In fact, there is real danger that associations of producers would aggravate rather than mitigate business slumps.

When prices in general show a tendency to drop, such associations usually urge their members to maintain the old prices. If the members heed this advice, output is restricted, unemployment within the industry is increased, and often surpluses of unsold goods pile up which eventually force down the price of the commodity. The net effect of the effort to preserve old prices is to delay necessary price adjustments and thus to prolong and aggravate the slump in business. If organizations within particular industries are to do more good than harm, a way must be found to prevent them from pursuing the disastrous price policies which have been typical in the past.

Equally great is the danger that associations of producers would aggravate, rather than solve, the problem of "sick" industries. By checking aggressive price cutting, these organizations would prolong the life of high-cost enterprises and, at the same time, attract more capital into the industry. Overdevelopment of industries can be prevented only by controlling the flow of capital into them and this must be done, in the main, by agencies outside of the particular industry.

Of more immediate promise than organizations of producers is a National Economic Council. But it, too, would have its limitations. To begin with, there are many things which would be pretty completely beyond the control of the Council. Among them are most of the international causes of depressions. Obviously a Council could have done little about many of the conditions which, during the last year, sent wheat, at Liverpool, down to the lowest. price in several centuries, coffee to the lowest price in a generation, or sugar, several weeks ago in Cuba, to an all-time low of less than nine-tenths of a cent a pound.

In the second place, the Economic Council, no matter how competent, would make many mistakes, and some of them would be serious. Consider the record of the principal control bodies that we now have—the Federal Reserve Board, the Federal Farm Board, the Interstate Commerce Commission. All of these bodies have done much good, but each has committed major errors. Many people believe that the Reserve Board was wrong in cutting the rediscount rate in 1927 and most people agree that it should have raised rediscount rates sooner and by a larger amount in 1928. Certainly the Farm Board committed a major error when, in the fall of 1929, it advised the farmers to hold their wheat. In fairness to the Board, however, it should be emphasized that *in the fall of 1929* most experts thought that the Board was right. The fact that the experts were wrong simply illustrates the difficulty of making correct decisions. Or consider the work of the Interstate Commerce Commission in devising a plan for consolidating the railroads. The Commission took nearly ten years to prepare a plan. It found the task difficult and even asked to be relieved of the responsibility. The scheme of consolidation eventually submitted by the Commission in the fall of 1929 proposed many systems which can only be described as grotesque.

Even the present depression is by no means solely the result of letting things take their course. On the contrary, it has been greatly aggravated by a multitude of errors in guiding economic activity—by unwise restrictions on exports, by Great Britain's attempt to stabilize the pound at too high a value, by unwise tariff increases, by mistakes in the policies of central banks, and by other national and international policies which could be cited. Indeed, the present depression furnishes many glaring examples of how disastrous may be the consequences of bad and unco-ordinated planning.

In the third place, the recommendations of a National Economic Council would often be defeated by the opposition of special interests. One of the gravest handicaps to business in the United States is our unscientific tariff. The tariff, as you well know, is not the result of impartial study of the economic needs of the country—it is the result of political "log rolling" and vote trading. If a few duties happen to be about right, that is purely accidental. And yet what an eruption of protest would arise from a host of special interests if an Economic Council dared to sponsor a revision carefully designed to reduce the burden which the tariff now inflicts on American business!

Suppose, again, that the Council were to attempt to check the overexpansion which almost invariably follows a period of abnormally large profits in an industry. When a few leading enterprises are conspicuously successful, the impression is created that easy money is to be made in the industry and, as a result, many poorly conceived and high-cost concerns succeed in obtaining funds from uncritical investors. Publication of figures on the productive capacity of the industry, on its output, and even on productive capacity under construction, would not entirely prevent this waste of capital. It might be substantially reduced, however, by requiring corporations to keep their accounts in a standard manner and to publish their financial condition at frequent intervals—as is now done by the railroads. Investors could then tell accurately which enterprises were making little or no profit. But suppose the Economic Council recommended that Congress require all corporations engaged in interstate commerce to submit to supervision and publicity of accounts. One can easily picture the fierce resistance that even this conservative proposal would arouse. Nevertheless, reliable publicity of accounts is of basic importance in guiding the investment of capital because, until it becomes a reality, the average security buyer will not know whether he is purchasing a share in a surplus or a share in a deficit, and vast sums will be wasted by being sunk in high-cost concerns.

Progress in controlling business cycles must hinge in large measure upon our success in reducing the violent fluctuations in the rate at which capital is invested. This can be accomplished only by substantially modifying present methods of saving and investing. In particular, it can be achieved only by controlling much more closely the expansion of commercial credit in anticipation of future saving. The stabilization of saving and investment is, indeed, one of the outstanding economic problems of the day, but the National Economic Council could not go far in attacking this problem without coming into conflict with some of the most powerful financial interests in the nation.

In the fourth place, the Council's recommendations would frequently be defeated by popular prejudice, ignorance, or misunderstanding. Suppose that such a council had been in existence in 1928 or 1929. By publishing statistical information or by issuing warnings, could it have curbed the frantic speculation in stocks? Could it have induced the Federal Reserve Board to act more vigorously and promptly in discouraging speculation? It will be recalled that, when the Reserve Board issued a warning against speculation in January, 1928, President Coolidge answered by expressing the opinion that brokers' loans were not too high but simply reflected the prosperity of the country. In the face of this statement from our chief executive would the National Economic Council have urged the Reserve Board to pursue a stronger policy in curbing speculation? And would the public, its appetite whetted by large paper profits, have paid attention to statistics or have tolerated a strong policy of restriction? It must be remembered that, so long as the public is winning, it objects strenuously to having the gambling game discouraged.

Suppose, once more, that an Economic Council had been in existence during the summer of 1930 when Congress raised the tariff. Little did the man in the street suspect that by raising our tariff we were starting a chain of events that, among other things, would later cause banks to fail throughout the nation. And yet this increase in our duties, with its disastrous effect upon foreign monetary and credit systems, accentuated the drop in world-prices which in large measure underlies all of our bank failures. Over one thousand economists urged the President to veto the tariff bill. Had an Economic Council been in existence in the summer of 1930, no doubt it would have pointed out dangers in the bill. But, in the face of the widespread popular ignorance concerning the tariff, is it reasonable to believe that the Council would have had any more influence upon either Congress or the President than did the thousand economists?

Let us come right down to the present. Suppose that an Economic Council were in existence today. Of just what use would it be in our present crisis? The world has built up an industrial system which operates upon a basis of credit. By a series of acts of almost unbelievable folly this country and other countries have been undermining the world credit system and thus reducing purchasing power. It is this steady disintegration of the credit system throughout the world which has made the depression so much longer and so much more severe than anyone expected. The causes for the disintegration of the credit system are numerous, but a major one has been the attempt of some nations to collect money which other nations cannot pay.

Little does the wheat raiser in Dakota or the cotton planter in Texas realize that he has more trouble in paying the mortgage on his farm because our government insists on collecting debts from the allies, and the allies, in turn, insist on collecting reparations from Germany. Nevertheless, that is true, for the attempts to collect reparations and war debts, by wrecking the world's credit system, have accentuated the drop in world-prices. Indeed, it is safe to say that no debts have ever been so costly to collect as those which the allies have collected from Germany and which the United States has collected from the allies. So ruinous have been these international payments that the United States could well afford to pay the allies not to pay us. And yet Congress, in approving the moratorium a few weeks ago, declared that we would not cancel the debts. If an Economic Council were in existence today, would it speak out plainly and tell the country that a resumption of payments would be ruinous? And should the Council so declare, could it dissipate the deep popular misunderstanding and prejudice that surround the subject of the debts and reparations? As long as this misunderstanding is so universal, will our government dare to pursue a rational policy with respect to the war debts?

I have pointed out four limitations of a National Economic Council—that many conditions would be beyond its control; that it would be wrong part of the time; that many of its recommendations would be defeated by hostile special interests; and that many would fail because of popular ignorance and prejudice. But these limitations do not mean that an Economic Council would be undesirable.

We are compelled to make a choice between two basic economic policies—either we may let events in the world of industry take their course without attempting to control them or we may face facts frankly, study them with care and discrimination, and endeavor, in some degree, to determine our economic fate. Surely we *must* adopt the second policy, for we dare not indefinitely trust things to take care of themselves.

But so complex is our industrial system and so great is the interdependence of its parts that we cannot hope to exercise control satisfactorily unless we acquire, in far greater degree than any democracy ever yet has done, the capacity to analyze facts dispassionately, to see behind the immediate consequences of economic policies to their ultimate results, and to take account of their effects upon the whole community as well as upon our own class or group. At present we are dangerously handicapped, in seeing facts plainly and in understanding our problems, by a heritage of ancient economic theories, well adapted to the days of small concerns but out of place today when enterprises count their capital by tens of millions and their employees by tens of thousands—theories which, in the name of liberty, defend the gross exploitation of workers and consumers and which teach us to regard gigantic concerns with hundreds of thousands of stockholders, not as public corporations, but simply as private businesses essentially no different from the neighborhood grocery store.

A National Economic Council would be simply a body for helping us to view our economic problems more realistically and to apply our intelligence to their solution more carefully, critically, and systematically. Its value would depend almost entirely upon the quality of its personnel. It would not be an important source of new ideas—no official body ever is—and it would not produce quick results. If it tried to accomplish too much, it would antagonize many special interests—some of great political power—and that might be its downfall. Nevertheless, if permitted to live and if composed of men of wisdom, courage, and broad sympathies, it should gradually raise the plane of economic thinking in the community and, by so doing, improve our capacity to manage our intricate industrial system and to control our economic destinies.

BIBLIOGRAPHY

SUGGESTED READINGS

I. For Beginning Readers

Calkins, Clinch, *Some Folks Won't Work*. Harcourt, 1930. $1.50.

Carver, T. N., *Principles of Political Economy*. Ginn, 1919. $1.50.

Chase, Stuart, *Men and Machines*. Macmillan, 1930. College edition, $1.75.

Clay, Henry, *Economics, An Introduction for the General Reader*. Macmillan, 1918. $2.50.

Hayward, W. R., and Johnson, G. W., *Story of Man's Work*. Minton, 1925. $2.00.

Johnson, Alvin, *Introduction to Economics* (revised and enlarged edition). Heath, 1922. $2.40.

Lynd, R. S., and Middletown, H. M., *A Study in Contemporary American Culture*. Harcourt, 1929. $5.00.

Marshall, L. C., and Lyon, L. S., *Our Economic Organization*. Macmillan, 1921. $1.68.

Pollak, K. M., and Tippet, Tom, *Your Job and Your Pay*. Vanguard, 1931. $2.00.

Slichter, Sumner H., *Modern Economic Society*. Holt, 1931. $5.00.

Soule, George H., Jr., *The Useful Art of Economics*. Macmillan, 1929. $2.00.

Thorp, Willard, *Economic Institutions* ("World Today Bookshelf"). Macmillan, 1928. $1.50.

II. Books on Some Special Aspects of Economic Life for Beginners

Black, J. D. and A. G., *Introduction to Production Economics*. Holt, 1926. $4.50.

Chase, Stuart, and Schlink, F. J., *Your Money's Worth*. Macmillan, 1927. $1.00.

Donham, Wallace B., *Business Adrift*. McGraw-Hill, 1931. $2.50.

Douglas, P. H., and Director, Aaron, *The Problem of Unemployment*. Macmillan, 1931. $3.50.

Filene, Edward A., and Wood, Charles W., *Successful Living in This Machine Age*. Simon and Schuster, 1931. $2.50.

Harper, Elsie D., *Out of a Job*. Woman's Press, 1931. $0.50.

PROPOSED ROADS TO ECONOMIC RECOVERY

Laidler, H. W., *Unemployment and Its Remedies*. League for Industrial Democracy, 1930. $0.15.

Lorwin, Lewis L., *Labor and Internationalism*. Brookings Institution, 1929. $3.00.

Lyon, L. S., *Making a Living*. Macmillan, 1926. $1.60.

Moulton, H. G., *The Financial Organization of Society* (third edition). University of Chicago Press, 1930. $4.00.

Patterson, E. M., *The World's Economic Dilemma*. McGraw-Hill, 1930. $3.50.

Tugwell, R. G., *Industry's Coming of Age*. Harcourt, 1927. $2.00.

Tugwell, R. G., Munro, Thomas, and Stryker, R. E., *American Economic Life* (third edition). Harcourt, 1930. $4.00.

Wallace, Benjamin B., and Edminster, Lynn R., *International Control of Raw Materials*. Brookings Institution, 1930. $3.50.

III. MORE ADVANCED GENERAL WORKS IN ECONOMICS

Bye, R. T., and Hewett, W. W., *Applied Economics*. Knopf, 1928. $3.75.

Davenport, H. J., *The Economics of Enterprise*. Macmillan, 1913. $3.25.

Edie, Lionel D., *Economics, Principles and Programs*. Crowell, 1926. $5.00.

Marshall, Alfred, *Principles of Economics* (eighth edition). Macmillan, 1920. $6.00.

Taussig, F. W., *Principles of Economics* (third edition). Macmillan, 1921. 2 vols., $3.00 each.

Taylor, Horace, *Making Goods and Making Money*. Macmillan, 1928. $2.50.

IV. MORE ADVANCED SPECIAL WORKS IN ECONOMICS

Angell, J. W., *The Recovery of Germany*. Yale University Press, 1929. $4.00.

Black, John D., *Agricultural Reform in the United States*. McGraw-Hill, 1929. $4.00.

Dewey, Davis R., *Financial History of the United States* (eleventh edition). Longmans, Green, 1931. $3.75, text edition $3.00.

Douglas, Paul H., *Real Wages in the United States*. Houghton, 1930. $7.50.

Edie, L. D., *Capital, the Money Market, and Gold*. University of Chicago Press, 1929. $0.50.

Ely, Richart T., *Elements of Land Economics*. Macmillan, 1924. $3.50.

Feis, Herbert, *Europe the World's Banker, 1870–1914*. Yale University Press, 1930. $5.00.

Gay, Edwin F., Mitchell, W. C., and Others, *Recent Economic Changes in the United States*. National Bureau of Economic Research, 1929. McGraw-Hill. 2 vols., $7.50.

(198)

BIBLIOGRAPHY

Hammond, J. L. and Barbara, *The Rise of Modern Industry*. Harcourt, 1926. $2.75.

Mitchell, W. C., *Business Cycles: The Problem and Its Setting*. National Bureau of Economic Research, 1927. $6.50.

Moulton, H. G., *Germany's Capacity To Pay*. Brookings Institution, 1923. $2.50.

Nourse, E. G., *American Agriculture and the European Market*. Brookings Institution, 1924. $2.50.

Reed, Harold, *Federal Reserve Policy, 1921–1930*. McGraw-Hill, 1930. $2.50.

V. Special Collateral Reading for Scheduled Addresses[1]

Atkins, McConnell, Edwards, Raushenbush, Friedrich, and Reed, *Economic Behavior: An Institutional Approach*. Houghton Mifflin, 1931. 2 vols., $8.50; students' edition, $6.00.

Black, John D., *Agricultural Reform in the United States*. McGraw-Hill, 1929. $4.00.

Carroll, Mollie Ray, *Unemployment Insurance in Germany*. Brookings Institution, 1929. $2.50.

Chamberlin, Wm. H., *The Soviet Planned Economic Order*. World Peace Foundation, 1931. $2.50.

Clark, F. E., *Principles of Marketing*. Macmillan, 1922. $3.00.

Clark, J. M., *Social Control of Business*. University of Chicago Press, 1926. $4.00.

Commons, John R., *Principles of Labor Legislation* (revised edition). Harper, 1927. $3.00.

Counts, George S., *The Soviet Challenge to America*. Day, 1931.

Hoover, Calvin B., *The Economic Life of Soviet Russia*. Macmillan, 1931. $3.00.

Keezer, D. M., and May, Stacy, *Public Control of Business*. Harper, 1930. $3.00, texts $2.25.

Laidler, Harry W., *Concentration of Control in American Industry*. Crowell, 1931. $3.75.

Lewis, Cleona, *The International Accounts*. Brookings Institution, 1927. $2.00.

Lorwin, Lewis L., *Advisory Economic Councils*. (Pamphlet Series), Brookings Institution, 1932. $0.50.

Nourse, Edwin G., and Knapp, Joseph G., *The Co-operative Marketing of Livestock*. Brookings Institution, 1931. $3.50.

---

[1] This list includes some titles applicable to the third group of addresses, to be delivered between March 19 and May 21, 1932.

Person, H. S. (editor), *Scientific Management in American Industry*. Harper, 1931. $6.00, text edition $4.00.

Rogers, J. H., *America Weighs Her Gold*. Yale University Press, 1931. $2.50.

Stewart, Bryce, *Unemployment Benefits in the United States*. Industrial Relations Counsellors, 1930. $7.50.

Survey-Graphic, March, 1932. "Economic Planning."

Taussig, F. W., *A Tariff History of the United States* (eighth edition). Putnam's, 1931.

Wolman, Leo, *Planning and Control of Public Works*. National Bureau of Economic Research, 1930. $3.00.

Wright, Philip G., *The Cuban Situation and Our Treaty Relations*. Brookings Institution, 1931. $2.50.

NEW SOCIAL RESPONSIBILITIES

OUR SOCIAL RESPONSIBILITIES

Walton H. Hamilton

IF I were to write the drama of the human race, I should cast Man in the rôle of Rip Van Winkle. Rip, you remember, went to sleep on the eve of important events; and, when he awoke, mistook the age in which he was living.

As age has followed age it has always been like that. The historian, looking back from some Olympian peak of the future, sees what has happened, knows what came of it, and tells how the human race has muddled along. But Man-the-Actor, in the world of here and now, must meet events head-on. He must confront situations as they come along without being told in advance what is about to happen. He sees with his mind, as well as with his eyes; he faces crises which are novel with the wisdom he already possesses, and that wisdom belongs to the past. In a period of change it is a product of an experience which is gone. As the new gradually emerges from the old, he persists—because he cannot help it—in dealing with the unfamiliar as if it were the familiar.

The people of the Renaissance saw their times, not as an era of creation, but as a revival of learning. The men of the Reformation indulged in the very real make-believe that they were merely freeing established religion of recent man-made abuses. To the folk who witnessed its coming it was many a decade before the Industrial Revolution was even a name. Man keeps on calling new things by old names—the work of the machine is manufacture; the contract of employment concerns masters and servants; the corporation, a device by which a group gets things done, is still a person. This business of letting new facts appear beneath old terms, of putting up new wine in old bottles, is necessary. Without it we could not easily live together in society nor could the stream of our culture run on without a break. But it also creates for us a confusion. As the world is hurried along toward its unknown future, the situation changes and our thought lags behind. Eventually the ideas in our heads get out of harmony with the facts of life.

In the endless drama of Man, Rip Van Winkle has appeared many times upon the stage. His act of sleep and awakening has run through many cycles. Just now he is emerging from a profound slumber. In Irving's story a new republic had come to claim Man's allegiance and yet the drowsy Rip still professed loyalty to His Majesty the King. Today a new industrial society has startled us into consciousness of its presence; and every man, awakened by the shock, has muttered his beliefs in the departed order of petty trade.

In fact, it is Man's social, rather than his individual, consciousness—the part of his mind given to the problems of the nation rather than to his own affairs—which has been at rest. He has made his personal accommodation to the novelties which have come along with surprising readiness. The great revolutionists of late have been inventors— such as Morse, Faraday, Edison, and Marconi; and business men—such as Carnegie, Rockefeller, Hill, and Ford. They have had the customary lack of respect of the revolutionist for the community of our fathers and the good old ways, and have transformed beyond recognition the world in which we live.

Yet Man was for only a little while automobile shy; within less than two decades the use of the motor car made mechanical knowledge almost universal. The strange thing called electricity has made over every activity of Man, yet its use has not stumped him; he has accepted, if not on faith at least with hope, the tortures of the radio. He has, with little difficulty, learned to bargain, rather than to plow; he has exchanged the old homestead for an urban flat; he has, without falling into bewilderment, submitted to such innovations as cash-and-carry, the chain store, instalment buying, advertising, and high-pressure salesmanship. He has even allowed his human nature to be more or less made over to fit his new environment. If given his chance, Man can, with ease and agility, make his personal peace with all the revolutionary novelties which science, industry, and business bring along.

It is in matters relating to our living and working together that Man has been in a doze. To him it is no "let's pretend," but a stern reality, that the older order of things exists. He believes, quite sincerely, that ours is an individualistic society, where each can take care of himself, and the devil may take the hindmost. So long as business is on the climb, income and employment are not too fitful, the stock market calls out a merry "Good Morning," and the word "prosperity" adorns party platforms and the newspapers, there seem to be no public problems. When business starts its decline, incomes begin to do the vanishing trick, bankruptcy and unemployment stalk the land, and executives command their employees not to use the word "depression," he becomes aware that the times are out of joint and that something ought to be done about it. So, in his rôle of Rip Van Winkle, he rubs the sleep out of his eyes and gathers up his stock of venerable ideas. Then, without bothering to inquire in what century he is living, he calls his outmoded common sense to the rescue.

Rip knows quite well how things worked when he went to sleep. His own gumption tells him how well they worked, and the very learned books, whose thought hails from the same bygone era, bear him out. The country is the land of opportunity; trades are open to all who care to enter them; chances for livings, for achievement, for wealth, are waiting for all who will take them. Each person must exhibit the cardinal virtues of diligence, sobriety, industry, and thrift. The requisites of success are finding one's own place, working hard, and saving. If one succeeds, it is by his own effort; if he fails, it is his own fault. The bankrupts are the inefficient; the owners of bad securities are fools who in any event would have been quickly separated from their money; the men and women without savings are the thriftless; the unemployed are the slothful and worthless. The be-all and the end-all of the economic problem is the once vital policy—now the empty creed—of rugged American individualism. In its terms social responsibility is the responsibility of every man for his own personal affairs.

All of these ideas—good hard common sense to the Rip who went to sleep—are today as outworn as the gristmill, the horse and buggy, and last year's hat. In ours, as in every society, the individual has dignity and importance and must have a chance and a place. But there does not exist today anything which Adam Smith would call "a system of natural liberty" or to which Mr. Jefferson would give the name "American individualism." The self-sufficient farm, upon which the family once produced its own living, is gone; gone, too, is the system of petty trade, by which necessities from afar and a trickle of luxuries were supplied.

The machine has created the factory; and specialization has brought about a division of labor on a continental scale. Now plants, factories, and establishments are crudely thrown together into industries, and industries are loosely articulated into a great industrial system. To this every man brings his labor or his property; from this every man fetches away the wherewithal of his living. Only in the sense that the law will not stop you are trades open to all who wish to enter. If you think yourself free to enter the industry of your choice—and may the better man win—try setting up as a realtor, or becoming a manufacturer of steel products, or starting a morning newspaper. You will discover that opportunity is hedged about with such requirements in the way of technical knowledge, capital, access to trained workers, and ability to wait, as to be open only to the favored few. Now that the solvent virtues of the mattress and the lady's stocking are no longer appreciated, the ordinary person, such as you or I, needs a technical knowledge of finance—such as recent events have proved that even many well-paid bankers do not possess—to be able to lay out his savings with safety.

If it is a mere job you want, you need not bother if you are an exceptional person or one favored of the gods. But if you are just one of many, it depends upon how many others there are and whether there are jobs enough to go around. Positions and incomes, opportunities and investments, no longer individual, have gotten tangled up with an economic order. And, to make it all the more confusing, the industrial system has fallen into the very habit which we condemn so roundly in individuals —it works fitfully and irregularly. At one time it absorbs the larger part, sometimes almost all, of its human and material resources; at another, with plants idling along and workingmen not employed, it behaves like a half-stalled machine. Yet, if one is to have a wage, or a living, or security, one must have a paying position or a remunerative investment somewhere within a great industrial system which is kept going. We have, without intending it— perhaps even without expecting it—given our chances at life into the keeping of a great collectivistic institution.

Yet, just awakened by the shock of depression, Rip Van Winkle tries to solve the problems of today as if they were those of yesterday. His very words are out of date; he speaks of corporate wealth as "private property"; of the formidable conditions one must accept, if one takes a job, or buys an automobile, or sends a telegram, as "freedom of contract"; of big business as "free enterprise"; and of leaving the industrial system without direction as "personal liberty." He uses the anti-trust laws to make national commerce behave as if it were petty trade; he is bothered because the turbulent forces of modern industrialism do not run in familiar channels. He talks about leaving control to "the natural laws of supply and demand"; he calls upon competition to make industries orderly and efficient, when the cases of oil and coal, banking and automobiles, present to his very eyes evidence of the losses and poverty, the disorder and waste, which attend its undirected operation.

Above all, Rip expects his less fortunate brother, aided if need be by a little benevolent charity, to find for himself a place, an income, and a living— even when there chance to be more workers than jobs. He cries, in the language of a pioneer society, for each to mind his own business, when the need is for such an ordering of the system upon which the livings of all of us depend that you and I and the next fellow have a real chance to look out for ourselves. So Rip Van Winkle wakes up, looks around, and begins to behave as if nothing had happened while he was asleep. The effect of it all is to demand something for nothing—to expect to have questions answered without even asking them.

As it is with each of us, so it is with the nation; in the world outside of fairyland we must pay a price for what we get. We must begin to concern ourselves with everybody's business and to put our house in order. This is to be achieved, neither by a return to the individualistic ways of our fathers, nor by a ready-made, hand-me-down, tight-and-tidy system, by whatever magical name it is called. Instead, the problem of control is at once comprehensive and detailed. We must do for the direction of the industrial system what has been, and is being, done with its technology. Our scientists and engineers, our discoverers and inventors, have created a new system of production; the men wise in such matters must create an organization for it. They must contrive and invent, arrange devices and procedure into schemes of control, and thus domesticate our rather unruly industrial machine. The depression has not created, it has merely revealed, our outstanding economic problem. It has thrown into sharp relief the lack of harmony between up-to-date processes of production and the out-of-date ways in which it is directed.

All of this means that our idea of social responsibility must be made over. It is not the ends, but the means, which demand a fresh outlook. We demand of our industrial system much the same things which our fathers demanded; if there is a difference it is that we are not so easily satisfied. But our mechanisms for getting them must be adapted to an industrial world which is different. The business system must be kept going with as little friction and with as much regularity as possible; this is an essential above all else. Our industries must perform a double duty—they must furnish to consumers an abundance of goods of a high quality at a reasonable price, and they must provide regular employment and adequate incomes to all the families who are dependent upon them for support. The older order of farm and petty trade, for all its niggardliness, did give security. The coming of industrialism has driven a line between Man and his means of livelihood. In the age of the machine, the corporation, and a world-market, we must have order that Man may regain his security. Without it "life, liberty, and property" will be at the caprice of untamed economic forces; with it as a foundation individuals may seek for themselves personal liberty and a way of life.

The depression reveals the current plight of our industrial culture. To see its lines in clear-cut relief we must look beneath the surface. In days that are gone economics was called "the dismal science." It taught that our natural resources were meager and the wants of an increasing population unlimited. The earthly doom of humanity was to beat out its life in poverty and misery against the walls of a prison-house. In days of the great industry it is Man's lack of control over things which gives the dismal tone to economics.

Today, in our concern with mechanisms like money and banking and our preoccupation with un-employment relief, we are prone to overlook the important and the obvious. We forget that we have as many fields and factories, as much of plant and equipment, as ample a supply of natural resources as we had in days of prosperity. Our capacity to produce has in no wise been diminished since nine-teen hundred and twenty-nine. If today laborers are out of work, productive wealth of many kinds like-wise stands idle. If workingmen are only partially employed, so are the establishments which produce the goods they would consume. At the quickening touch of organization laborers and production re-sources can be made to keep each other going. Nor need we be content with even the standards of life which we enjoyed just before the great decline. We can today control our numbers; what our natural

resources are—and whether limited or unlimited—
we do not know; for natural resources depend upon
what our knowledge and our industrial arts make
of them. In this year of grace we face a dilemma
which is a national challenge. We are, almost all of
us, possessed of inadequate livings; yet the industrial system has an unused capacity to produce
which is prodigious. The task is to convert unused
capacity into usable goods. The truth, the plain
truth, the simple truth, is that the stuff for an economic order which is an instrument of national
well-being is all here; as the decades go by, it can
be made to yield us better and better livings. The
problem is one of order and of direction. In short,
our economic order has passed from a deficit to a
surplus economy—from a dismal to a hopeful
economy. Its riddles are not to be unlocked by the
venerable notions in the head of the Rip Van
Winkle who went to sleep.

Like the surface of the earth, our culture has its
fault lines. It is along the lines of these breaks that
disturbances are likely to come. A social order is
not secure when its technical processes belong to the
twentieth century and its means of order to the
eighteenth. We need to take our cue from the lov-
able character in Irving's story; for Rip Van Winkle
was no "dumb-bell," and he did eventually wake
up.

AMERICAN STANDARDS

Frances Perkins

AN ECONOMIC depression makes a frontal attack on the standard of living. Consider the significance of what Jane Addams told us in an earlier radio talk concerning the thirty children who in one month were known to have come back to one school in the Hull House district, after having joyfully left some years before to live in the suburbs, where their parents hoped to achieve home ownership and independence. Much praise belongs to the Long Island town which prevented the wiping out of a class of small-home owners, thus protecting a worthy class of unemployed and sustaining the property values and standards of the community. Not only in property holdings and wage income, but in health, in education, in hope and self-respect, in family unity, is there a lowering of standards during a depression, often with bitter fruits that appear and reappear down through the years.

The standard of living has always been regarded by intelligent labor leaders as an important element in their struggle. Their philosophy was: Push up the standard of living. Hold gains at any cost.

The standard of living was recognized by economists of a generation ago as having significance in stimulating production. The stock story is of the importation of movies to Africa as a method of giving the natives some spending urge as a reason for steady work.

More recently, industrialists and bankers, with the shift to large-scale production, have recognized in a high standard of living the possibility of greater mass consumption and, therefore, of a great United States of America market of wage earners, farmers, small business men, and professional workers. A continually rising standard of living has been depended on by those industrialists to furnish a market for automobiles, electric refrigerators, radios, and the host of new and improved products which have been forced on the market in bewildering array and ever increasing quantities. Advertising and salesmanship widened the market. Now this depression has narrowed the market, thus sowing the seeds of its own continuance.

The part played by the standard of living in our social life and organization becomes more apparent as we consider housing, food, clothing, recreation, self-improvement, security, and the other elements that enter into it. An American standard of living is understood to include adequate housing with sufficient air, space, privacy, conveniences, and respectability to make the finer things of life possible. Such common conveniences as bathrooms, sunlight, fly screens, heat in winter, we feel that we must have.

At the same time the rapid changes characteristic of our industries are discouraging to home ownership.

In food the standard goes considerably beyond the mere absence of hunger. It includes a pleasing variety, with fairly liberal allowance for meat, vegetables, fruits, and dairy products—in short, all that is required for physical well-being, energy, and alertness. In our choice of foods we now recognize dietary principles. The school children of today understand the functions of vitamines and would not willingly omit them from their diet.

In the matter of clothing, perhaps, the American standard is most characteristic. The lack of class distinctions and social barriers, the Americanization of vast contingents from all the lands under the sun, the feverish haste to rise in the social scale, have all led to emphasis on the importance of expenditure on clothes, with slavish following of the rapid caprices of style. It is a matter of amazement how quickly the $300 dress on 57th Street is copied in the $8.00 dress on 14th Street. Clothing is a membership ticket to the circles in which one wishes to move; it is an added shelter which, unlike the home, cannot be unknown to one's friends and business associates; it is a form of recreation and as such is an alternative to the concert or theater; it favors the making of the right contacts for advancement and for marriage with those having a like standard of living. If a person of high standard of living marries one with a low standard of living, the result is not always sound from the standpoint of the proper functioning of the family as a social and economic unit.

Among the moderately well-to-do the expenditure for rent, fuel, and light is roughly about two-tenths of the family income. Food requires three-tenths, and about two-tenths is spent on clothing. This leaves three-tenths for house furnishings and miscellaneous. A moment's reflection will show the growing importance of the miscellaneous group. The item of cleanliness under modern urban conditions must include not only soap and running water, but the washing machine and the vacuum cleaner, the laundry bill and the cost of dry cleaning. That vague but important classification, "miscellaneous," also includes savings, health expenditures (such as doctors and dentists), special education, and recreation. Recreation is essential to the good life. Much could be said concerning the high cost of recreation. Under the present system it is generally not the spontaneous production of social relations.

We hear much concerning the cost of living, but the truth is that no satisfactory estimate of the cost of living is available. The United States Bureau of Labor Statistics made very conservative estimates some years ago. For an industrial worker with wife and three children in New York City the estimate was roughly $1,800 to $2,000. Today the same scale could theoretically be maintained for somewhat less. The irony of the situation, however, is that today the wage earner is probably supporting his brother-in-law, and cannot get the benefit of a reduced rent without moving, which would cost more than the amount saved. There is a great and pressing need for an up-to-date, comprehensive survey of the cost of living, representing both the United States as a whole and separate regions therein.

In comparing American and European standards of living there are misunderstandings that need to be cleared up. In the first place, comparisons have been made between union wage rates in this country and union wage rates in England, Germany, and other European countries, without stopping to consider that the American figures are weighted out of all proportion by the building crafts, whose hourly wage rates run about twice those of the corresponding rates in manufacturing.

Second, not enough allowance has been made for the greater violence of the swings of the business cycle in this country and of the custom of throwing men on the scrap heap at an earlier age. It is not wage rates alone that count but annual income and life-income.

Third, more allowance should be made for things that do not come inside the pay envelope. Who can measure the worth to the European worker of his unquestioned right to bargain collectively, or of his sickness insurance, his unemployment insurance, his old-age pension, and of the subsidized theater and opera, of the unbelievably inexpensive expeditions for his children to the centers of culture, of the forest preserves organized for his own week-end outings, of the cities governed scientifically by experts? The fact that the countries of northwestern Europe are not sending their full contingent of immigrants as permitted by our laws suggests that the economic differential is not as great as has been assumed.

In appraising the American standard, it is well not to be misled by averages. The Pullman porter told the English traveler that the average tip was a dollar, but then he added that "there's hardly anybody that pays the average." In particular it is necessary to take note of four things. First, differential against the unskilled, who receive less than two-thirds that of the skilled, is greater here than abroad. Second, the wage levels both for skilled and unskilled are distinctly low in the South as compared with the North. Third, there are depressed industries in this country as truly as in England—coal mining, for example—where the earnings are small and irregular. Fourth, the security implied by social insurance is largely absent.

It is important to recognize on the one hand the strategic social importance of the standard of living and on the other how narrow is the margin of the best of our actual standards over what is socially necessary, while great sections of our working population are below such a standard. It is necessary to visualize a major economic depression as a frontal attack on the standards of living. *During the upswing of the business cycle wage rates lag behind living costs, and during the downswing the general wage income declines faster than living costs.*

(219)

The standard of living suffers, also, a rear attack in some of the necessary expedients adopted to meet the emergency conditions. Thus, in my state, there is the setting of a maximum of $15 a week in relief, and the practice of staggering work among those who retain their jobs.

The standard of living cannot survive a permanent policy of curtailing production. Rather, through wise planning, there must be full production and full employment, with shortening of hours not to limit production but to raise the standard of living. During emergency conditions there is a real shortage of jobs, but in the long run labor creates the product from which, often, labor can be put to work and paid.

Real protection of the standard of living requires that backward regions and backward industries be brought up to the desirable social level.

Greater recognition must be given to the element of economic security, a new recognition of the importance of status. It has been said that the progress of civilization is the development from status to contract. Rather we should say it is the progress from status based on birth to status based on contract. This is the significance of the employment-reserve plan of the General Electric Company, for example.

With this emphasis on security must go a greater emphasis on the inner standard of living, the things that make life worth living. Otherwise we shall merely have improved methods of achieving unimproved ends. The use of the radio not for advertising but for a series of discussions of our vital problems is a recognition of the importance of the ideals and standards that are within.

And, finally, the standard of living should be thought of as ever rising. It is a flying goal. Borrowing the slogan of the American Standards Association, "Standardization is dynamic, not static. It means not to stand still, but to move forward together."

SOCIAL INSURANCE

Paul H. Douglas

THE typical American of a century ago in the northern and middle-western states was a small farmer and as such was not exposed to many of the risks which the modern industrial worker experiences. Handwork was almost universal, the speed of labor less, and accidents in consequence were relatively few. Even when a worker was thus laid up, the farmwork could generally go on in some fashion through the labor of other members of his family. This was also the case when the worker was disabled because of sickness. When he grew old, he still had his farm and could do work in proportion to his strength. There was, therefore, a more or less solid basis of protection upon which a worker could fall back.

The situation today is quite different. The typical American now works for wages either in manufacturing, mining, transportation, building, or commerce. In the first three of these groups of occupations, the work is with machinery, and in all the tempo of industry is markedly swifter. If the wage earner has to stop work because of accident or illness, his income stops also; and when he is too old to keep up to the pace, he is dropped and finds it difficult to exercise such abilities as he still possesses.

If we add to all this the interruptions of working-class income which result from his being thrown out of work because of seasonal fluctuations, business depressions, and technical changes, we can see how severe are the risks to which he is exposed.

Now the wages which the modern workers receive are, even in the United States, too scanty in terms of modern living standards to enable them individually to accumulate a sufficient reserve against these risks. The average annual earnings of some fourteen million non-agricultural wage and clerical workers in 1928, according to my computations, amounted to only $1,504—or an average of but $29 a week. When we remember that this was an average, we realize that a very large percentage must have received less than this figure.

Thus, last July, the average starting rate for unskilled labor in the country as a whole was, according to the United States Bureau of Labor Statistics, 41.2 cents an hour. If the unskilled, therefore, had been employed for 10 hours a day, which is appreciably more than the average length of the working day, their daily wage would have been only $4.12, and, if they had not missed a working day, their yearly income would have been 306 times this figure, or $1,260. This would have been a weekly average of only a little over $24. But $24, we should remember, was considerably above the average actual earnings of this class of labor because of shorter working days, short-time, illness, and unemployment.

When we realize that the Chicago Council of Social Agencies, in their carefully planned budget, fixed a scale as a basis for relief to dependent families which in 1929 would have amounted to $1,370 for a family of five and to $1,980 for a self-supporting family, we see how inadequate the wages of a large percentage of our workers actually are. Miss Leila Houghteling, indeed, discovered after a thorough study of the incomes and expenditures of the families of nearly four hundred unskilled and semi-skilled workers in Chicago, that the earnings of the heads of the families were in 70 per cent of the cases insufficient to support their actual dependents on the scale recommended by the charities for dependent cases, and that even when all sources of family income were considered, the total income was insufficient in 45 per cent of the cases.

While conditions are, of course, somewhat better in the smaller communities, it is evident, I take it, that an individual worker generally cannot accumulate a sufficient stake to protect. himself against losses which he may possibly suffer from accidents, sickness, and unemployment—nor provide an adequate reserve against indigent old age. These risks, therefore, yearly sweep multitudes of families into destitution and misery.

It was virtually inevitable, then, that society should move in the direction of throwing some protection around the workers to help replace that which they formerly possessed. During the last half-century, therefore, the industrial countries of the world have come increasingly to provide social insurance against these great risks of accidents, ill health, old age, and even unemployment. This social insurance differs from private voluntary insurance in at least two essentials: (1) Society regards protection against these risks as so important that it either makes insurance against them a compulsory matter or, at the very least, heavily subsidizes any voluntary efforts which are made by the workers to meet them. (2) Society recognizes that the interests of its members are to a large degree mutual, and therefore distributes the expense in part so that the heavier burdens may fall on the shoulders of those who are better able to bear them.

Protection against industrial accidents was the first type of social insurance to be generally adopted. After having been put into operation by virtually all of the European countries, this form of insurance was provided by forty-four American states during the decade 1911–20. Formerly workmen and their families could only recover from employers for accidents or death if the personal negligence of the employers was clearly established and then only after a long and costly lawsuit, in which the employers could use the three common-law defenses of contributory negligence of the worker, assumption of risk by the worker, and the negligence of a fellow-servant. The workmen's compensation laws have changed all this. They aim to compensate the worker for all accidents incurred during the course of employment unless wilfully caused by him, and to do this without the former delays and expense of the legal process.

Even those who originally opposed the passage of these acts now admit that they have served a good purpose. Unfortunately, however, the benefits granted are still inadequate, amounting to only 50 per cent of the wages in fifteen states, and never exceeding 67 per cent. Even more important are the maximum weekly limits to the amounts which can be paid, which very commonly reduce these percentages still further, and the fact that nearly half of the states limit death benefits to six years or less and also fix very inadequate limits to the amounts which can be paid for permanent total disability and for the loss of such vital members as arms, legs, and eyes. From various investigations which have been made, though in some cases not yet published, it has also been established that in certain states many of the injured and their families, because of their need for immediate funds, have signed away their rights to full legal payment in return for very much smaller lump sums and direct settlements on the part of the accident casualty companies. We need, therefore, improvements in both legislation and administration if the compensation laws are really to fulfil their purpose.

Until recently, workmen's compensation was the only type of social insurance provided by our states. In recent years a few states have begun to take action upon a second of the great risks, namely, that of indigent old age. This problem is becoming more acute from a number of causes. In the first place, improved public health and the decrease in immigration are rapidly increasing the proportion of our population formed by old people. Whereas in 1870 only 3 per cent of the population were sixty-five years of age and over, by 1930 no less than 5.4 per cent were in this group.

The population shift from rural to urban centers has, moreover, made it more difficult for these older workers to find employment, as is evidenced by the fact that while 74 per cent of those in this age group were gainfully employed in 1900, only 60 per cent were so occupied in 1920. It is, moreover, probable, although confirmation awaits complete official analysis of the Census returns for 1930, that during the last decade the possibilities for the employment of the older-age workers within our cities have also narrowed. The decline during the last decade in the numbers employed in manufacturing naturally resulted in the dropping of many of the older men and women, and this was probably contributed to by the higher accident rates which characterize these workers, and by the higher premiums to which they were liable under group-insurance plans.

The two chief types of social protection which at present exist for the aged are: (1) public poor relief, which generally takes the form of the poorhouse, and (2) the voluntary pension plans of private employers. The humiliation attendant upon the first deters large numbers from applying for assistance who are in dire need, while it is in addition an extremely expensive method of caring for the indigent. Thus a study by the United States Bureau of Labor Statistics in 1925 of over 2,000 almshouses showed an average maintenance cost per inmate of $335. In addition, there was an average investment in land and buildings of approximately $1,750 for each of the 86,000 inmates. At 6 per cent this amounts to an average capital cost of $105, and adding this to the maintenance cost gives an average total cost of $440.

Private pension plans are necessarily limited in scope, since they are scarcely applicable to the smaller establishments, and can in the nature of the case only include those who have been employed for a long period of time with a particular company. Furthermore, since these pensions are regarded by the courts as gratuities rather than as deferred wages, it is always possible for the companies, if they find the expense of the system to be onerous, to alter the terms in favor of themselves. The result is that the workers or pensioners cannot be certain that they will obtain the provisional benefits. Since most of the private pension plans are actuarially unsound and if carried through will cost industry very much more than was originally believed, it can be seen that this is a very shaky reed for the minority under such plans to lean upon for protection.

To help meet this situation a number of states have passed some form of old-age-pension law, of which the best examples are those of California, Massachusetts, New York, and Delaware. Of the approximately 80,000 aged who are now in receipt of pensions, about 90 per cent are in these four states. These measures are mandatory upon the counties instead of being optional as was the case with the earlier and more defective laws, but the expense is borne by the states as well as by the counties. In this way the expense is distributed over a wider area than the county itself, so that the wealthier counties may help to bear the burdens of the poorer. The counties, however, are given an incentive to refrain from excessive expenditure, since if this occurs they will have to pay part of the cost. The state, because of its grants, will in turn be enabled to lay down certain minimum standards of efficiency.

These acts almost universally establish seventy years as the minimum pensionable age. The pensions are not to be automatic and universal but are paid only to those whose private income is insufficient to maintain them upon a minimum scale and whose children or other near relatives are unable to support them. By these means, family responsibility is maintained and the relief given to those who need it. Most of the state laws limit the pensions to $30 a month, although the Massachusetts and New York laws, which now include about three-fourths of the total pensions, fix no definite limit. Where such a limit is fixed, however, the amount of the public pension diminishes proportionately as the private income of the pensioner increases.

The interest in old-age protection is growing and further action by many additional states is badly needed. Virtually all of the other industrial nations of the world protect old age by some form of self-respecting pensions or social insurance, and we should not continue to be laggards. Although the present laws are non-contributory, it is quite possible that many of them may ultimately be placed on a contributory basis. If the age of eligibility were to be reduced to sixty-five years, as is to be hoped, it is possible that the added expense might, for example, be met by contributions from both the employers and the workers. Since the existing and maturing crop of old people has not, however, had the chance to make contributions in the past, it will nevertheless be necessary for some time to take care of the aged on a non-contributory basis.

The third great risk, that of illness, is one which is almost universally provided for in Europe, where nearly seventy million workers are protected by compulsory plans and several million more by subsidized voluntary measures. European systems provide two types of benefits, cash and medical. While the former was originally much more stressed than the latter, an increasing amount of the funds are now being spent for medical and hospital care. A movement for a similar system in the United States was defeated some twelve to fifteen years ago because of an imperfect understanding by the public of its real purposes and because of the opposition which it aroused from almost mutually contradictory sources. The succeeding years have brought a clearer understanding of the burden of illness upon the worker and the heavy cost of severe illness.

It is well known that both sickness and death rates are much higher among the poorer than among the well-to-do sections of the population. The workers suffer greatly from the loss of earnings during the time they are ill. If the father of a family is ill, the mother is commonly forced to seek work away from home, children are taken out of school and sent to work in order to repair the family fortunes, and in a large percentage of the cases the family becomes either partially or wholly dependent. They are commonly unable to afford adequate medical attention and a vicious circle sets in. Illness makes the family still poorer and then poverty and lack of medical care still further impair health.

It is necessary, therefore, to protect the wage-earners' incomes during these periods of illness and to provide medical care. The burden of caring for such sickness on the part of the poor cannot properly be allowed to rest on the medical profession, and a much more satisfactory system of financing medical care is needed. This should provide more attention and skilled treatment for the workers, and at the same time safeguard the medical fraternity's legitimate claims to professional freedom and reasonable compensation. Some system of pooled contributions is needed to effect this and to provide both cash benefits and some form of self-respecting collective protection against the costs of medical and hospital care.

The last of the "Four Horsemen" of industrial risks is unemployment, a disease which challenges the intelligence and good will of our whole society. The application of the theory of social insurance to this grave social ailment will be discussed in this series next week.

UNEMPLOYMENT INSURANCE

John R. Commons

NO SUBJECT except banking has command-
ed more attention during the past two
years than unemployment insurance. The
reasons are evident. A cycle of business prosperity
with full employment, followed by a depression
with millions of unemployed. These cycles have
been repeating themselves for a hundred years, but
never before have employers begun to feel responsibility for their own employees. Besides these cycles
there has been an unprecedented laying off of employees on account of machinery and mechanical
power, to which is added seasonal unemployment.
A few large firms have voluntarily started unemployment insurance, but in Europe the governments
themselves have been compelled to pay unemployment benefits on account of the imminent danger of
revolutions.

Different countries naturally lean toward different
methods of unemployment insurance according to
their social emergencies, their industrial traditions,
their national psychology, and their form of government.

The system of state-operated unemployment insurance in force in Great Britain has one serious
weakness which most Americans wish to see avoid-

ed in establishing unemployment insurance schemes in this country. It may be illustrated as follows. The British employer who furnishes fifty-two weeks' full employment pays fifty-two premiums on his pay-roll, but the employer who furnishes only twenty-six weeks' employment pays only twenty-six premiums. Both payments are made into a common insurance fund. By this device of a common fund the employer who stabilizes his employment in reality pays a bonus to the employees of his competitor who does not stabilize his employment.

The American idea is just the opposite. The employer who furnishes fifty-two weeks' employment would pay no premiums whatever and no unemployment benefits to anybody. But the employer who gives only twenty-six weeks' employment would be required to pay twenty-six premiums in order to pay unemployment benefits only to his own employees.

The British system, so far as the employer is concerned, really penalizes the employer who stabilizes employment. The predominant American plan, which is not a nation-wide scheme but fundamentally only an unemployment-reserve plan for the individual establishment, offers an inducement of higher profit to the employer who stabilizes his employment, and would impose a penalty of lower profits on the employer who does not stabilize, by requiring him to pay premiums into his own establishment fund and pay benefits out of that fund to his own unemployed.

The American plan appeals to the individualism

of American capitalists, who do not want to be burdened with the inefficiencies or misfortunes of other capitalists, and it fits the public policy of a capitalistic nation which uses the profit motive to prevent unemployment.

It must be realized, however, that the American plan is not as advantageous as the British to the unemployed workers, just because it does not draw upon the efficient employers to pay benefits to employees of the inefficient employer. Consequently, where unemployment insurance is established in this country, the employees of plants which work irregularly go without unemployment benefits when the reserve funds are exhausted. In every case where a dispute arises the workers demand an insurance fund because they are interested in relief more than prevention, but the employers stand for establishment funds because they do not wish to pay for the losses of their competitors.

The American plan is similar to a policy such as that of workmen's accident insurance in those states that give a merit rating, in the form of lower premiums, to employers who have a low accident rating. But this, as provided at first in the British unemployment insurance, does not get any of the expected results toward unemployment prevention, and has been abandoned, because no merit rating can possibly be calculated for so fluctuating a misfortune as unemployment.

The American plan, however, works automatically without merit rating, because there is no common fund to which all contribute, but only a shop fund. Each establishment determines for itself how much its profits may be increased by stabilization of its own employment or reduced by its own failure to stabilize.

I can best illustrate the practical working of the American plan by the unemployment-compensation law, known by the name of its sponsor, the Groves Law, recently adopted by the state of Wisconsin, after ten years' drafting, redrafting, and improvement on the first bill introduced a decade ago. It is practically the same as the bill recommended by Governor Roosevelt for the state of New York. The law is fashioned avowedly on the unemployment-reserve plans adopted during the past six years by a few far-sighted corporations, such as the men's clothing industry of Chicago, the General Electric Company, and the nineteen co-operating employers of Rochester, New York.

The Wisconsin law requires only that employers shall set up establishment funds and provides for no common fund administered either by the state or by an employers' mutual insurance company. The law does not provide for contributions by the workers or by the state, because it is reasoned that neither the state nor the employees can do anything whatever to prevent unemployment. The employers alone, under this theory, are in a position to prevent unemployment, because they are alone responsible for management. And the only effective method by which they can be induced to prevent unemployment is by making the system operate on profits.

Even so it is recognized at several points in the Wisconsin law that the responsibility to which employers can reasonably be held is very limited. The law applies only to employers with ten or more employees, partly because it has been found that the largest instability of employment is in the larger establishments, and partly because it is felt that small employers cannot be expected to devise means of prevention more than they are now doing.

The law also excludes all establishments which operate less than four months a year, which practically excludes those markedly seasonal industries, like pea canning, which operate usually less than four months in the year. It further excludes employees receiving more than $1,500 per year, and there are several other exclusions. The state government and subordinate cities and counties, however, come under the same rules as the private employers.

The Wisconsin law, furthermore, places the premiums to be paid by employers at what may seem the ridiculously low figure of 2 per cent on the payroll, and places the limit of benefits at one-half the lost wages for a period limited to ten weeks. Evidently 2 per cent is not enough to build up reserve funds or pay benefits anywhere near approaching these maximum benefits of the law.

Thus this law cannot possibly be called a relief measure and cannot possibly take care of all the unemployed, as would have been the case if it had been an insurance law like the British and German laws. The German law has high total premiums of 6 per cent of the pay-roll, paid jointly by employers, employees, and the state. Both in Great Britain and Germany, moreover, there are extra benefits paid by the state in periods of business depression. The Groves Law is only a moderate prevention law, not calculated to provide adequate relief in periods of abnormal unemployment.

But one thing must be noted about this very low premium of 2 per cent on the pay-roll which will be paid by employers in Wisconsin. It represents an insignificant increase in the cost of production, amounting probably to not more than 1 per cent of the cost of production. However, it can be shown, from the federal income-tax reports, that the average margin for profit for some 60,000 manufacturing corporations is usually less than 3 per cent per year of sales income available for dividends after all costs are paid. It follows that a 1 per cent increase in cost of production is, on the average, 33 per cent of the margin for profit on sales.

This represents a very decided inducement to the average employer to prevent unemployment. Of course, for many corporations the margin for profit is larger than 3 per cent, but it is doubtful whether a state can successfully place by law a general tax on employers exceeding 30 per cent of the average margin for profit.

The important thing is that employers should begin to set their minds to work on the prevention of unemployment by all the well-known devices, such as efficient employment exchanges, diversification of product, staggering employment, not hiring more employees than they can expect to retain, and so on. The psychological effect of the Wisconsin law will be more important than the puny contribution figure of 2 per cent of the pay-roll, because it operates on the margin for profit. Such, at least, has been the effect of the workmen's accident-compensation laws —which, although the premiums are low, have done more than ever was done before in creating the "safety spirit" which reduces premiums by preventing accidents. We need now an "employment spirit," and to enact legislation, like the Groves Bill, which will help to create an employment spirit, like the safety spirit.

The Wisconsin act goes far toward creating an employment spirit, by favoring voluntary systems if they provide benefits to employees and costs to employers not less than those of the compulsory system. One company has already announced a voluntary system whereby the employer pays 5 per cent and the employees 5 per cent. This is a higher contribution rate, permitting higher and longer benefits, than is found under any known system of unemployment insurance.

If employees contribute they should not be compelled to do so by law, and are not so compelled by the Wisconsin law, though they may agree voluntarily with their employers to contribute, in order to increase the relief features of the system. And if employers set up voluntary systems it is reasonable to expect that they will go beyond the compulsory 2 per cent of the law.

I have spoken about the failure of the Wisconsin law to protect those engaged in seasonal industries. But by far the greatest cause of unemployment is the general inflations and deflations of prices which no employer and no state, perhaps not even the federal government, can prevent. Nevertheless, the evident responsibility for unemployment compensation, during long-continued depressions like the present, lies on the federal government.

Unemployment insurance and the prevention of unemployment are undoubtedly the greatest of the new social responsibilities that must be assumed. Our capitalistic system of huge corporations is causing more unemployment than the older neighborhood and agricultural system. It is a miserable paradox that the richest country of the world should not be able to feed and clothe its workers when they are eager to work. The principle of unemployment insurance is simple enough. It merely provides that, during periods of prosperity, there should be set aside enough reserves to at least feed and clothe those who produce the wealth of the nation. Big corporations, during the past ten years, have learned to set aside reserves for dividends. They have an even greater responsibility—a social responsibility —to set aside reserves for unemployment. And if the unemployment is so great and long continued that employers cannot assume the total responsibility, there is no place to impose the responsibility except upon the nation as a whole.

Of course, prevention of unemployment is better than unemployment relief or insurance. But the greatest motive to prevent unemployment is so to adjust insurance legislation that employers can make more profit by prevention than by insurance.

LAND UTILIZATION

M. L. WILSON

FROM what has been said before in this series of talks it is clear that agriculture as well as industry must have a new economic philosophy, and that the nation must adopt a system of planned land use. Otherwise, I believe, farming is doomed to a condition, which, call it what you may, will be little better than peasantry.

The continual general decline in price levels, since November, 1929, has simply broadened the base of a depression which the farmer had known for a decade. The price of his wheat has dropped to the lowest point since the time of Queen Elizabeth. The depression has brought him five-cent cotton, twelve-cent eggs, twenty-three-cent butterfat, thirteen-cent wool, thirty-two-cent corn, and three and one-half cents a pound for hogs.

Taking the 1909–14 price averages as 100, present index levels are as follows: wholesale prices, all commodities, 98; all farm products, 60; things which farmers must buy, 121; taxes which farmers must pay, 266. Much lower prices for what he sells, higher prices for what he buys, and still higher taxes—this is what Russian peasants a few years ago called "the scissors." Here are the upper and nether millstones, slowly but surely grinding the life out of rural America.

The results? Farm foreclosures, tax delinquencies, and overwhelming debts unprecedented in the history of this country—and the end is not yet. Family farms with generations of ancestral ownership are moving into other hands because of unpaid debts and taxes. To the cities this means that one-third of the population cannot buy what industries and cities have to sell.

Fortunately there is a way out, but the way demands a reversal of the basic land policy of this nation. Free land and its accompanying democratic ideal of a farm and a home for everyone has been the corner stone of American rural progress and philosophy for the past century. Now, suddenly, the problem has changed from how to get land into production to how to get some of it out of production. The answer to this fundamental problem in my mind lies in a national system of land-use planning.

At the outset I may say that I believe that land-use planning must be the foundation for any farm-relief program. At the same time, neither this nor any combination of plans can be successful with a wobbling monetary system that forces farmers to pay their obligations with three times the amount of farm produce that the obligations represented when they were contracted.

I present six steps which I regard as essential to a land-use-planning program:

First, Congress should immediately repeal the Homestead Act, together with other free-land laws and enact a new national land-policy bill.

There is no land remaining in the public domain

suitable for farm development and home building. The repeal of the Homestead Act, perhaps the greatest, as well as the most sentimental, of all our historic land laws, would be a striking symbol of the official close of the epoch of free land and limitless agricultural expansion. Congress should pass a new land-policy bill embodying national land-use planning, federal-state land relationships, conservation of land resources, and adjustment of the agricultural plant to national needs.

Second, each state should immediately classify its lands, develop a state land-use plan, and institute a program of action.

The colleges of agriculture and the state experiment stations in co-operation with the United States Department of Agriculture should immediately press forward reliable surveys and studies of soils, topography, climate, and records of past crop yields. Farm history; economic, marketing, and farm-management material should be brought up to date, to show the family incomes, standards of living, and status of schools. The use of the land would be determined by the facts obtained. The work need not be done in minute detail, for much material of this type is now available and only needs correlation. If it were made a major project the essential work could be done in a year.

The New York state program of land utilization is a good example of what I have in mind. Of it Dr. Ladd of the New York College of Agriculture says:

It is the land policy of the state of New York to differentiate closely between its different classes of farm land. The land which is clearly suited for permanent agricultural use shall be developed as highly and as intensively as possible with hard-surface roads, electric power, good high schools, and health facilities available for every farm as fast as these are economically possible; the land which is unfitted for permanent agricultural use shall be transferred from private to public ownership and be used for growing trees, furnishing recreational opportunities, water-supply protection, beautification of the state, and timber production. Stated more concisely, the land policy of New York consists of three things—first, classification of the land; second, developing the best land as highly as possible; and third, transferring the poorer land to public ownership and reforesting.

The third of the steps which I regard as essential is that poor land, as determined by the land-utilization studies, be taken out of farm production. That this fundamental part of the new land policy of the nation has already been incorporated into the thinking of high governmental officials, completely reversing the old expansion policy, is indicated by the following quotation from the 1930 report of the Secretary of Agriculture:

It should be an essential aim of our agricultural policy to facilitate the withdrawal from agriculture areas that seem likely to remain unprofitable. Public provisions should be made for the utilization of this land for purposes other than farming. Public ownership of land that cannot possibly be farmed would in many areas mean a better economic use of the lands in question and also do something to relieve the pressure of unneeded production upon our markets.

Furthermore, when New York state passed a twenty-million-dollar bond issue for the purchase of sub-marginal land, it set a significant and far-reaching example for taking poor land out of the production picture. Sub-marginal land in this discussion is that land which cannot pay taxes and yield a fair standard of living. It must be recognized, of course, that changing population, changing food and clothing habits, and other factors which have to do with changes in markets and consumption determine what is and what is not submarginal land.

The fourth step which I suggest is that land taxes should be modified and, where necessary, local rural government reorganized.

Most of our local governmental units were created in the horse-and-buggy days. The telephone, automobile, and good roads have rendered many present governmental units too small, resulting in duplication, unnecessary expense, and inefficiency. In such cases consolidation of units and managerial forms of administration will make the tax dollar go much farther. The general property tax is likewise a carry-over from a simple society. Modification and change in our land-tax system, also a relic of bygone times, are necessary before many improvements in land utilization can be effected.

The fifth step is solution of the problem of the surplus on the good lands. The withdrawal of poor lands from production will help but by no means solve the problem of the surplus. The surpluses of wheat, cotton, tobacco, corn in the form of lard, and certain fruits, come largely from the good land. The withdrawal of inferior land in the greatest amount that we could possibly expect would still leave an area of superior land which today is producing a surplus above the profitable demand of the present depressed markets. Moreover, this area of superior land is capable of producing in the future a price-depressing surplus unless production is held under control by some system of planned-farming administration. To determine the scale of operations in accordance with which even the staple products of American farms are produced would be a tremendous undertaking. However, the general outlines of a workable plan have been set forth under the name of the "Domestic-Allotment Plan," and this proposal has been subjected to enough discussion so that its essential features have been reasonably well determined.

In brief, the domestic-allotment plan calls for the issuance of certain allotments to farmers to grow a certain number of acres of the kind of crops they have been growing, the farmer to receive tariff protection for the products from his allotted acres. He would be at liberty to grow more but this would be without tariff benefit.

The allotment plan is similar to the production-adjustment measures proposed for industry by Mr. Swope and the United States Chamber of Commerce. Essentially it is in line with labor's plan for reducing working hours and maintaining constant employment. The allotment system calls for careful planning of agricultural production of the nation with state and regional programs fitting into the general national plan.

The plan is simply a means for applying tariff protection to farm products of which we produce a surplus. It is different from proposals incorporating equalization-fee or export-debenture features in that it has a positive device for preventing undue expansion when prices rise. Certainly it would appear that the American farmer might be willing to sacrifice a little of his vaunted independence for a system of allotments and planning if he could gain material economic benefits.

Good lands, as producers of surpluses, now are a part of the world-economy, and the plans made for them will depend upon whether they are to continue as a part of the world-economy or whether they are to be regarded from the viewpoint of a strictly national economy.

During the past ten years, when changes in international economic relations have caused acute distress to the producers of surplus crops in this country, farmers and Congress have made one effort after another. But the surplus-producing farmers are worse off than ever.

It is becoming more and more apparent that in this dilemma only two roads are open, neither of which has been tried. One road is marked "open and unrestricted trade—produce for the markets of the world"; and the other, "high tariffs—adjust production to the markets of the nation."

Before the World War, Europe was to our farmers a great, hungry mouth which took all the agricultural products it could get. The world-economic structure then was in fairly good working order; tariffs were relatively low; international exchange of commodities took place easily. But what a change since the war! Higher and still higher tariffs; nations striving to produce their own food; import quotas; war debts; international ill will. If the United States should take the first-mentioned road, the now closed mouth of Europe might again be opened to the products of good lands of the United States by reducing tariffs, canceling or adjusting war debts, and joining the League of Nations to foster peace and good will. With the European mouth open, the farmers on the good lands would only ask to be left alone to work as hard, to till as much land, and to roll up as big harvests as they pleased. The combination of the best land in the world, highly mechanized farms, superior efficiency, and a high level of intelligence, I believe, would enable the farmers of the United States to compete on equal terms with any nation.

But many farmers, when they scrutinize this road, shake their heads and say "No." They want high tariffs; they insist that Europe must pay her debts just as farmers must pay theirs; and they believe that the United States should attend to its own business. This means the other road and is essentially the policy of today. If it is to be continued the nation must adopt a system of land-use planning for its good lands so that production may be balanced with the market demands of this nation. Otherwise I see nothing but continued chaos.

To balance production, and to make land-use planning effective, it will be necessary, perhaps, to have compulsory pooling, or a domestic-allotment system as I have described. Compulsory pooling, while greatly at variance with our farm individualism, is being tried in more than twenty countries and seems to fit in with extreme nationalistic policies.

The last step in the program which I recommend

is part-time farming and decentralization of industry.

Since this program contemplates releasing families from poor agricultural lands it is logical to ask: Will these join the already overcrowded ranks of the unemployed? They will unless industry also adopts a new policy. That a new policy is in the making is indicated by the fact that some industries already have started a program of decentralization which is coupling industry with small-farm agriculture. In one state 60,000 workers live on small farms surrounding towns and cities.

If this is to become a policy for the nation, definite planning is necessary. Instead of letting this movement proceed as it will, it should be guided and directed into channels which will bring maximum employment and maximum enjoyment for the people. In an industrial world part-time farming will mean greater security for the workers and constructive employment for leisure time.

Small farms of this kind would not produce the great food staples of which there are now a surplus and, therefore, would not effect production on the good lands.

I have briefly sketched how the idea of economic planning is being applied to agriculture and land use and how it is giving a new and hopeful approach to the difficult farm problem. If farmers will accept the planning idea and the program that goes with it there is great hope for rising standards of farm living. But this acceptance requires a recognition by farmers that they are part of a complex world. Their problems are those of the middle period of the twentieth century. Agriculture and land-use planning will not work with the frontier farm individualism of the eighteen eighties and nineties.

During the past year there has been much abstract talk about economic planning and its academic aspects. I am inclined to think that there has been more practical and experimental progress with the idea in agriculture than in any other industry. Agriculture is starting to make national land-use plans.

At the instigation of the state colleges of agriculture, and of the Secretary of Agriculture, there has been set up a National Land-Use Planning Council composed of representatives of all federal departments and bureaus dealing with land policies together with representatives of the state colleges of agriculture. This national council has the support and advice of a National Advisory Committee composed of representatives of the national farm organizations, farm co-operatives, the National Chamber of Commerce, and other national organizations interested in land policies. The National Council is attempting to co-ordinate governmental activities in administration, research, and fact-finding and thus develop some real national land-use planning. Farm interests were responsible for having the first bill introduced into Congress dealing with economic planning—the Christgau Bill, introduced in 1930, for regional readjustments in agricultural production, to assist in preventing the production of undesirable surpluses.

These are signs that agriculture is getting ready to plan.

CO-OPERATION AS A STABILIZING FORCE IN AGRICULTURE

Chris L. Christensen

MODERN society, in all its commercial, industrial, and social complexities, is based upon the willingness of individuals to unite in combined effort. Co-operative effort not only makes possible our great commercial undertakings; it is also the foundation of our institutions of government—local, state, and national—as well as of our organized educational, religious, and welfare enterprises.

The mutual interest that brings people together in corporate enterprises, which have become such an important part of our industrial life, is nothing more nor less than the desire and willingness to co-operate. Modern business, in practically all its forms, is based upon, and functions through, group effort. Co-operative organization is merely one form of such group activity.

Frequently my duties take me to a middle-western town where on each visit I pause to admire a beautiful stone building which shelters a co-operative enterprise—a large and successful mutual insurance company organized and conducted by hardware dealers.

Not infrequently in arranging for large gatherings at our institution I have occasion to deal with passenger associations which have been organized to handle, for the several railroads, certain matters of common concern.

One might multiply, without end, examples of co-operative or group effort, organized, and carried on, for the single purpose of meeting more adequately the needs of some urban or rural group. But it is needless to do so, for the more one analyzes the complexity of modern society the more likely is he to accept the view that co-operation among individuals and among groups is an inevitable development. Co-operation is the very essence and price of progress.

This working together for better economic ends and conditions is generally recognized as "good business." In this way economies and efficiencies supplant sentiment and tradition. A group of dealers organize to conduct a mutual hardware insurance company for no other reason than to effect economies and to develop certain efficiencies. Similarly, officials of railroad companies find it to their advantage to perform certain services through agencies which they control in common.

And so it is with farmers; whether it be in the marketing of farm products, for the purpose of securing credit, or in the buying of farm supplies, they often find it to their economic advantage to act collectively. Through co-operative organization the farmer becomes a participant and partner in a group business enterprise, planned and carried on to render a more efficient and effective service in the production, manufacturing, storing, and marketing of products, and in the purchasing of supplies.

Co-operative organization among farmers is just as logical an economic development as is corporate or group effort among urban business men or groups interested in manufacturing, finance, and commerce. Agricultural co-operation has become necessary because of the growth of specialization in production; and by reason of the enlargement of the market area in which the farmer sells. The pioneer farmer had little need and opportunity for joining with his fellows in disposing of his products. His market was confined largely to the community in which he lived. He produced, on his farm, practically all of the food and clothing which his family required. His purchases were few.

But the American farm of today is far from a self-sufficing unit. Agricultural conditions have changed. The average farmer today is producing farm commodities for distant markets. Since the days of our pioneer farming, farm marketing has grown from a simple process of exchange between neighbors into an intricate system in which various marketing functions have become necessary. Today, there is a multiplicity of marketing services to be performed in getting beef, or wheat, or oranges, or milk products from producer to consumer. These marketing functions may include assembling, grading, manufacturing, financing, storing, transporting, selling, and finally distributing the commodity in small lots to the ultimate consumer.

Certainly the farmer has reason to be more interested than anyone else in the efficient marketing of his products. Indeed, it would be difficult to contend that marketing is not an important part of the farmer's business. Every loss and every waste, occurring between him and the ultimate consumer, is likely to be carried back to him in the form of a decreased demand for his product or an added cost in marketing. In either case the result is a lower net return to himself, to his community, to his commodity group, and to his industry.

The farmer is, therefore, vitally interested in every phase of marketing, but as an individual he can do little to improve his marketing practices. As a member of an organized group, however, he can help to bring about improvement in marketing technique.

To the farmer who sells to a country buyer this transaction is the beginning and end of the marketing process. Improvement in the grade and in the quality of his commodity and the adjustment of his production to market demand have little practical meaning to him. When, however, he becomes one of an organized group, he begins to understand the relation of his production practices to more economical marketing and to better prices. He learns something of the demand for his products and something of the factors which affect the prices received. Because he sees the necessity of making changes and appreciates the effect which they may have on his income, he is helped to make, voluntarily, adjustments and improvements in his production practices.

It is only through active participation in his cooperative organization that the farmer is in a position to know, first hand, the needs and desires of consumers and to adjust his production to meet such demand.

Thus he may learn that the consumer prefers a standardized, dependable quality product, and that it is to his advantage to grade and pack his product before selling it. He may learn that the highest quality product is in so much greater demand than is one of average quality that it will pay him to undertake the extra trouble and expense involved in producing only the best.

Furthermore, the individual farmer working alone is in no position to cope on equal terms with organized groups in finance, manufacturing, transportation, and commerce. It is true that the prices of agricultural products are influenced, in large measure, by supply and demand, but it is equally true that efficient organization can exert an influence upon these conditions: An apple crop in the hands of thousands of farmers may be thrown on the market in such quantities as to demoralize the market. The same crop in the hands of a few strong organizations with unified programs may be handled so as to have a stabilizing influence on the market.

When we realize that there are 6,250,000 farmers in the United States we understand more fully some of the profound weaknesses which result from following an individualistic or an every-man-for-himself policy in farm marketing. Of the 6,250,000 individual farm producing units in the United States, approximately 1,300,000 are producing wheat; about 1,900,000 are growing cotton; over 1,500,000 may be classed as dairy farmers, while another 1,000,000 are raising other kinds of live stock; approximately 430,000 are growing wool and mutton; and fully 225,000 are growing fruits and vegetables.

If these millions of isolated farmers are to exercise better control of the marketing of their products it will be necessary for the producers of the various commodities to work together under qualified leadership.

Co-operative organization among American farmers has passed through its inspirational and its legalistic stages and has evolved into a practical business. Farmers, today, are no longer greatly concerned with the moral and theoretical concepts of co-operation, but are inclined to an ever increasing extent to judge its merits on the basis of practical business results.

Co-operative managers and directors are devising ways in which farm group efforts can be made more efficient. In consequence, co-operative associations are growing in management experience, in financial strength, and in the confidence of their members. Farmers have quite generally gotten away from the idea that by organizing they can arbitrarily fix the prices of their products. They are more and more coming to realize that the advantages of their organization must come from improved business methods—standardization of handling methods, sound and adequate financial policies, efficient management, and skilful merchandising.

There is a growing appreciation that the extent to which farm co-operatives take advantage of their opportunities will be in proportion to the responsibility which farmers assume toward these organizations. They know now that there is nothing mysterious about the co-operative method of doing business and that co-operation possesses no supernatural powers. It succeeds only when it is organized to fill an economic need, is ably managed, soundly and adequately financed, and intelligently supported by its members.

We must all appreciate that business institutions of the magnitude of some of our large farm co-operatives do not develop without cause nor continue to exist except by virtue of services rendered. There have been very definite reasons for the growth of these business associations among farmers, and for the attainment of their present strength.

When it comes to the application of co-operative organization methods to the millions of farming units in this country, we see that there are three principles which serve to guide co-operative effort. In the first place, farmers generally form *local* co-operative units. For instance, grain growers organize around local grain elevators. Dairymen organize around local creamery, cheese factory, and milk plants. Fruit and vegetable growers organize local assembling and packing plants, and live-stock producers organize in community areas and around terminal markets.

A second characteristic of organization among farmers is that they organize along *commodity* lines. This is perfectly natural and would appear to be a sound type of organization procedure. Farmers producing the same commodity certainly have a common interest, and there is obvious economy in using the same facilities and skilled personnel in assembling a large volume of the same commodity for the purpose of grading, processing, and preparing for market.

A third characteristic of co-operation among farmers is that local units, handling the same commodity, usually *federate* into larger units for the purpose of financing, storaging, selling, and distributing.

Co-operative organization among farmers along these lines serves as a stabilizing influence in many ways.

The formation and functioning of local co-operatives serve as stabilizing forces for their members and their communities. When there is federation of a large number of local co-operatives, with common problems and interests in a commodity, there is also an enlarged opportunity for dealing with larger problems and economic forces within that particular commodity industry.

The organization of individual farms—in local units and commodity federations—enables farmers to deal on a more equal basis with other organized groups in industry, commerce, transportation, and finance.

Co-operative organization serves to improve the quality of farm products. Members are paid market premiums received by their association for products of superior quality. Consequently they have an incentive to employ better methods. The California citrus growers reduced to two their large number of varieties of oranges in order to supply the trade with a uniform quality throughout the year. This is effective stabilization.

Co-operative organization helps in the formulation and adoption of standards resulting in uniform grades, packs, and packages. The apple growers in the northwest states have, by united effort, succeeded in establishing grades and packs known for their excellence throughout the nation and in foreign countries.

Co-operative organization serves as a wholesome and effective competitive force—resulting in increased efficiency in assembling, processing, manufacturing, transporting, storing, and distributing methods and practices. Several thousand dairy farmers in the north-central states, through their co-operative association, have built up a nation-wide organization for the sale and distribution of high-quality dairy products under their own brand.

Co-operative organization can serve to acquaint groups of individual farm producers with market conditions and consumers' preferences and demands. With this information, supported by the services of strong co-operatives, growers may then adjust their farm practices so as to produce the kind and quality of products that best satisfy market demands.

Co-operative milk organizations have succeeded in adjusting seasonal production to consumption requirements in the particular market in which they are operating. While this involves adjustments in the milk production on each individual farm, the benefit derived from such adjustments repays the effort involved in making them.

These are some of the ways by which co-operative associations are able to exert stabilizing influences upon the production and distribution of farm products. In my estimation continued progress lies in these directions, in building upon these firm foundations, rather than through monopolistic control or by any other method of direct price fixing.

TECHNOLOGY AND BIG BUSINESS

Harlow S. Person

IN A power station not far from my office is a
turbine which generates 2,000,000 man power.
The latest machine in a floor-cover plant can
produce 10 miles of 6-foot-wide linoleum, and a
modern steel rolling mill over 450 miles of bars,
each in a 24-hour day. A mechanized oven enables
two men to bake 4,000 loaves of bread per hour. A
factory in Milwaukee has made for the automobile
industry over 10,000 chassis frames per day with a
scant 200 men, of whom only 50 handle the product.
High-powered machines do the work as men manip-
ulate levers. Ever larger, more efficient power-
energized equipment has increased the productivity
of labor. In the ten years following the war total
physical productivity of American industry advanced about 50 per cent, and physical productivity
per wage earner a few points more. That is not all
the story. It is a conservative estimate that, if
equipment were utilized to capacity, we could
double the quantity of physical goods produced in
a working day. These fragmentary facts indicate
one great contribution of engineering.

The other great contribution of engineering is a
new technology of management. An economist has
said recently that the greatest event of the nine-

teenth century was when Frederick W. Taylor began at Midvale those experiments in measuring and organizing work which led to scientific management. But for the influence of scientific management in industry, modern large plants with highly productive equipment would not be practicable from the business point of view. The quantities of materials to be purchased, handled, and processed, the volume and variety of orders to be met, the number and variety of operations to be co-ordinated, would have brought about confusion more costly than the gains resulting from the greater capacity of equipment, were it not for the precision and economy of scientific management's organization, measurement, standardization, and planned control of operations. Industry now manages modern huge plants more effectively than it formerly managed small plants of relatively toy machines.

Note well, however, that this excellence of management relates to the internal affairs of enterprises and not to their external relations.

Scientific, impersonal, creative, engineering has embodied the powers of nature and the craft skills of man in equipment for production and devised effective methods for their management. It has made relative plenty possible. If plenty is not realized, responsibility rests not upon the creators of such devices, but upon all of us for the manner in which we have permitted them to be misused.

There have been indications of a fitful progress toward plenty. The upward trends of productivity and of realized income have recently been so marked as to lead to prophesy of "a new economic era of prosperity." Yet today, instead of well-distributed plenty, the standard of living all over the world is declining and tens of millions of people are without work and in want. Confidence has been shaken, pride humbled, social morale shattered.

For us two ominous facts stand out! One is the plunge from intense activity to present unemployment of some 8,000,000 American workers. The other is the fact that between 1920 and 1928, when productivity was mounting to unprecedented heights, there was a shrinkage of over 2,250,000 in the number of people gainfully employed in the major industries and agriculture. We are applying mechanization in such a manner as to deny a share in its operation and in the results to an ever increasing proportion of the population.

It is sometimes convenient to make a distinction between gradual, or technological, unemployment and sudden loss of work during depression, or cyclic unemployment; but both represent the effect of unregulated application of machine technology. Technological unemployment is gradual displacement much of which is permanent; cyclic unemployment is technological unemployment periodically intensified.

There is a traditional assumption that labor released slowly by technical progress is fairly promptly reabsorbed into industry. This may have been a reasonable assumption in a period of flexible pioneer industry, free natural resources, and an increasing purchasing power, much of which was derived from sources other than manufacturing income. However, it does not fit the facts of our industry, which is more mature and in many ways less flexible. There is not time to go into the reasons given by economists. It will, perhaps, be of greater interest to note the judgment of a leader who knows from long experience what technological development means to employment.

Myron C. Taylor, Chairman of the Board of the United States Steel Corporation, in an address before the Boston Chamber of Commerce on March 24, declared that because of inevitable further mechanization of industry he found it difficult to see how the large number of workers now in industrial centers could continue to get work at fair compensation, and that many would have to become agricultural laborers. If we grant Mr. Taylor's premise that production and employment must be stabilized within the present framework of managerial policy and practice, the conclusion that even in good times there will be net reduction in employment is inescapable. Some of us, however, do not grant the premise.

We have time tonight to note three fundamental reasons why mechanization of industry as now managed causes both gradually increasing and periodically intensified unemployment.

In the first place, the profits motive, unrestrained, has found in technological change both the incentive and the opportunity to manifest itself in a manner which causes instability. Industry has gradually been led away from the primary objective of production of goods for need, with profit as an incidental reward, to production of money profits for capitalization, with production of goods as an incidental means. This is "big business." Just as in pioneer days industry capitalized future income expected from permanent growth of population and of consumption, so now it capitalizes, as though permanent, abnormal income acquired from the utilization of cost-reducing equipment. When a new industry or a more productive technology in an established industry comes into being, there is a rush into the enterprise for the purpose of capitalizing beyond actual investment the initial surplus profit of the new enterprise or technology. The surplus profit is employed in part, under competitive pressure, in technological improvement, in part in inducing, but at a diminishing rate of return on the expense, consumption beyond the point of spontaneous demand, and in part as a basis for stock-splitting and other forms of overcapitalization.

There is consequently loaded upon industry a great overhead of obligations which are inflexible and imperious. To meet these obligations and to maintain investment values, prices, although sometimes reduced slightly under pressure of competition, are not reduced in proportion to the economies effected by improved equipment and methods. The result of such inflation and price maintenance is reduced purchasing power as compared with the total value placed on the increased product. Eventually there appears, at first, of course, only here and there, the inability to meet obligations. This occasional insolvency, because of sensitive interrelations between enterprises, spreads rapidly like the leak in a dike and undermines the entire structure. Thus progress in technology stimulates the cycle, involving speculative opportunity, excess saving and investment, increased production capacity, reduced costs, maintenance or raising of prices, overcapitalization of surplus profits, excessive overhead of inflated fixed obligations, pyramided sales expenses, relative decrease in consumer purchasing power, and, finally, industrial demoralization.

In the second place, as a whole industry has not been organized, which is one reason for the unrestrained play of the profits motive. We have striven to prevent even spontaneous organization. In a few instances the control which organization can establish is apparent, as in the case of the railroads and the steel industry. Generally individual enterprisers plunge unrestrained into the promotion of new establishments and into acquisition of new equipment without serious regard for the effect on employment in their own plants, and without any regard for the effect of accelerated obsolescence on employment in competitors' plants.

It has been believed that laissez faire is necessary to stimulate enterprise and insure social progress, and that the efforts and losses of individual managements are a small price to pay for progress. This was probably true of pioneering industry appropriating and exploiting abundant natural resources. Relative to the social gain the sum of individual costs was small, for the dice were loaded in favor of the enterpriser. When industry has become mature and the relationships within it complicated and sensitive, as they are today, particularly with respect to the growing overhead of fixed costs, the errors of individual activities are multiplied rather than merely added together, and the product is a social cost so great that periodically the industrial structure is shaken as by an earthquake. Accordingly we stand idle today while the accountants and receivers are eliminating weak members and rearranging the remaining parts of the structure, and while the government is shoring up the sagging overhead with public funds.

In the third place, there is no planning of the development of industry and of the relations and activities of its constituent parts so as to assure social welfare—everybody employed and relative plenty for all. Planning is necessary in a private enterprise if it is to function properly and survive. The larger the enterprise the more necessary is organized planning. Yet we expect the greatest enterprise of all—national industry—to function properly without planning. The automobile industry is a striking illustration of the waste of such neglect. We have permitted to be constructed a national plant with capacity to produce 9,000,000 cars annually. Present sales are approximately 2,000,000. Sales will undoubtedly fail to approximate capacity at any time in the near future; a large part of the investment will become obsolete, and perhaps half the workers now released will never be re-employed by the industry. All for want of social control and planning.

None of the principles of that excellent management which engineering has given private enterprise has been applied to industry as a whole. Yet this must be done to avert collapse and chaos. The first step in that direction will be of as great significance as was that other first step taken by Frederick W. Taylor fifty years ago.

Industrial leaders have recognized the necessity of stabilization of production and of employment, and have formulated their plans. But these plans do not promise stability plus plenty. The assumptions in current industrial thinking were boldly expounded by Myron C. Taylor in his recent Boston address as follows: "Controlled production may be expected to come about automatically, as our surplus stocks become exhausted, and as competition, spurred by necessity, discards obsolescent production equipment and adopts justifiable price control that sacrifices some part of production volume to secure reasonable price levels for commodities." This is what the formulated plans really propose, only they do not rely on automaticity but suggest social sanction. Their proposals mean stability through labor-eliminating machinery, reduced pay-roll and other costs, restricted production, the tariff, and price maintenance! Stability for the workers retained by industry, but not for those dismissed to peasant farming! A pseudo-stability designed to maintain the value of existing and future overhead and its claims on social income, but not stability to produce abundantly for need!

I prefer a plan of different type, such as is represented in bills which have been introduced into the present Congress by Senator LaFollette and Representative Person. These look toward stability through social control of industry, and production for need by means of a planned and regulated employment of all willing workers and a maximum utilization of the new technology; stability plus plenty and increased leisure for the art of living.

There is no escaping the responsibility of two choices. One is the choice between the chaos of laissez faire and organized stability. The other choice, if stability is chosen, is between stability without plenty and stability with plenty. These choices now confronting us are the most momentous in our history.

TRENDS TOWARD CONCENTRATION

Harry W. Laidler

IT HAS now been about a half-century since the people of the United States first had their attention called to the movement toward concentration of industrial control in this country.

Up to the eighties of the last century, most Americans took it for granted that America was, and would continue to be, a country of the small business man. In the beginning of the Republic, if we ignore for the time being the slave economy of the South, we were largely a nation of small farmers and traders and artisans and frontiersmen. As the years advanced, however, steam power gradually took the place of hand power and bigger and better machines were introduced into our industrial life.

The increasing expensiveness of these machines, the ever expanding markets, and other forces made it necessary for the individual business man to get capital from outside sources. So business men formed partnerships. They organized corporations. They enlarged the small corporation into the middle-sized and the large corporate unit. They came into conflict with other business men who were doing the same thing. Bitter competitive warfare ensued, frequently followed by "pools" or "gentlemen's agreements." These soon gave way to trusts of the older type, in which a group of trustees were allowed to hold the property of formerly competing firms. A pioneer among these trusts was the Standard Oil trust, organized in 1879. The sugar, the whiskey, the lead, the linseed oil, and other trusts rapidly followed.

As might be expected, the organization of these monopolies led to vigorous attacks and, finally, to the passage of anti-trust laws, the most famous of which was the Sherman Anti-Trust Law of 1890. The enactment of these laws helped to bring the trust movement to a temporary standstill.

Beginning, however, with the campaign year of 1896, which witnessed the defeat of William Jennings Bryan and the victory of William McKinley, a second combination movement set in. In this second period, the older form of trust was discarded, while a new type of holding company took its place. During the next seven or eight years, this new merger movement carried all before it and, by 1904, John Moody was able to record a list of over three hundred combinations, seventy-eight of which, according to Moody, controlled over half of the production in their respective fields.

A mighty wave of protest followed in the wake of these combinations. Leading articles condemning the steel, the beef, and other trusts appeared in the principal magazines. Theodore Roosevelt began to wield his "big stick" against the "malefactors of great wealth" and, in 1904, the Supreme Court dissolved the Northern Securities Company, the great railroad holding company of the West.

Again the merger movement slowed up and the average citizen began to give his attention to other developments. Then followed various Supreme Court decisions in the United States Steel and other cases, permitting the continuance of these great corporations. Mere size and *potential* monopoly, declared the Court, were not in themselves to be regarded as illegal.

In the meanwhile came the World War. During the war, the United States permitted and even encouraged co-operation between corporations such as was previously regarded as utterly illegal. Following the war, the country passed through the depression of 1921 and then through the boom days ending in the Wall Street crash of 1929, boom days which presented to many an opportunity to float industrial and financial securities unparalleled in the history of the country. During this period, a third merger movement took place, more extensive than any of its predecessors.

The results of this merger movement are not yet fully tabulated. Some facts, however, are known. We know from the researches of Dr. Willard Thorp and others that, in manufacturing and mining, over seven thousand firms were merged or acquired between 1919 and 1928 inclusive. We know that, in the public-utilities field, the number of mergers increased from twenty-two in 1919 to over a thousand in 1926. We know that in banking and in retail distribution the movement toward the big industrial and financial unit went forward with almost lightning rapidity.

By 1929, according to Doctors Berle and Means of Columbia, some two hundred corporations controlled nearly one-half of the wealth of the nonfinancial corporations of the country and over two-fifths of corporate income. If recent trends of growth were to continue, declare these authors, by 1950 "80 per cent of non-financial wealth would be in the hands of these two hundred non-financial corporations."[1]

Our public utilities have long been, for the most part, local monopolies. They are now, in many cases, virtual national monopolies. The Bell Telephone system collects about seven out of every eight pennies spent in the United States for telephone service. The Western Union Telegraph Company does about four-fifths of the telegraph business. A small group of holding companies control the major part of the electricity generated in the United States. In the case of one electrical holding company, according to the Federal Trade Commission, the ownership of a million dollars worth of stock at the top of the pyramid is sufficient to control as much as three hundred and seventy million dollars worth of stock in the operating companies at the base of the pyramid.

In mining and manufacturing, we find many industries in which one corporation controls one-half

---

[1] *American Economic Review* (March, 1931), p. 10.

to nine-tenths of the business or wealth in their respective lines of activity. This is true in the case of iron-ore reserves, nickel, aluminum, farm machinery, shoe machinery, sewing machines, cash registers, cameras, Pullman cars, and such food products as soup, crackers, chewing gum, yeast, etc. In other lines—automobiles, steel, cigarettes, electrical machinery, passenger cars, etc.—two corporations occupy a major portion of the field. In still other industries, three or four great overlords dominate. Our entertainment is being handed out to us increasingly by movie and advertising and radio organizations. While in banking, 1 per cent of the banks of the country now possess resources equal to those of the other 99 per cent.

Even in retail marketing, formerly the stronghold of the independent storekeeper, big business has come to stay. Ten chain-store corporations each did a business in a recent year of a hundred million dollars, while one grocery corporation, possessor of 16,000 stores, has an annual trade of over a billion dollars a year.

When a person speaks of concentration of control, it is often pointed out that this concentration has been accompanied in many industries by a wide distribution of stock ownership among customers, employees, and the general public. This, of course, is true, although the trend has often been exaggerated. However, as Professor William Z. Ripley of Harvard has pointed out, as stock ownership becomes more scattered, the tendency is to concentrate control ever more tightly in the hands of management. If eight or ten interests each control large blocks of stocks in a corporation, these eight or ten are likely to be actively represented at its annual meeting. Where there are hundreds and thousands of owners, however, the individual stockholder who owns one or two shares of stock is likely to do little more than sign a proxy giving an officer of the corporation the right to vote for him. The officers gather these thousands of proxies and virtually dictate the corporation's policies. Where the mass of stockholders are allowed to buy only non-voting stock, dictation by the inner group is even a simpler matter.

Practically every student of the subject admits that the present industrial situation, with its centralized control, is a highly dangerous one to the people of the country. Under it, the few possess irresponsible power over the lives of the masses and have used that power, in many cases, to the detriment of consumer, producer, and investor. It is a tragic fact that, outside of the railroads, the great corporations have, in but rare instances, permitted the organization of bona fide trade unions. And yet everyone knows that no equality in bargaining power is possible between an individual wage-earner and a billion-dollar corporation. This lack of organization is undoubtedly one of the reasons why the real wages of industrial wage-earners increased by around 2 per cent a year between 1922 and 1929, while industrial profits increased at the rate of around 7 per cent a year.

(275)

The merger movement has been accompanied by an extensive propaganda campaign in behalf of these giant corporations. It has been accompanied by gross inequalities of income and wealth that bear little or no relation to differences in ability, and by wild speculation, tragic insecurity, and vast industrial wastes.

Increasingly people are urging that something be done about this situation. Three lines of action are proposed. One proposal is that, whenever this trend leads to private monopoly, the monopoly be dissolved and an effort be made to return to free or regulated competition. Those urging this action see few economic advantages in monopolized industry and feel that it has developed largely as a result of unfair competitive practices and bad court decisions. They would seek to enforce the anti-trust laws and put more teeth into them.

The second group of citizens maintains that it is impossible to return to competition. Free competition, it declares, was only a passing phase of capitalism and logically gives rise to combination. To say that combination resulted from illegitimate practices is to tell only a part of the story. The movement must also be explained, among other things, in terms of the revolution in machinery, and in commercial and financial practices, and a desire to avoid wastes and bankruptcy. Nor were the days of free competition days of plenty or freedom for the masses. Moreover, the need of the day is not more competition, but more social planning. This school points to government regulation or to industrial co-ordination by the industry as the way out.

A third school, composed of Socialists and others, agrees that it is practically impossible to unscramble these scrambled industrial eggs. This school, however, declares that the question is becoming a question between private monopoly and public monopoly in many lines of industry. It points to the failure of most of our regulation of utilities to protect the masses.

The regulated, the members of this group declare, are constantly seeking to regulate the regulators. They cite the statement of Joseph P. Eastman of the Interstate Commerce Commission that, at least in utilities, public ownership is the way out. They feel that democratic control, reward according to merit, industrial security, and genuine social planning are only possible where the community owns its great basic industries.

They believe that the trend toward concentration is preparing the soil for social ownership by reducing the number of corporations in many industries to a handful and by developing increasing numbers of administrators in industry who depend upon a salary, rather than upon profit, for their chief incentive. For the profit goes largely to the inactive stockholder.

They declare that, as industry becomes more complex, it is ever more difficult for the ordinary citizen to invest his savings safely or wisely from the standpoint of social needs and that, if we are to bring

about a proper balance between our power to produce and our power to consume, society must take
an increasing share in the direction of investments.

They favor a public ownership which would give
adequate representation to consumers, technical
staff, and wage-earners on boards of directors and
they point out that, in education, in health, in recreation, in water supply, in highway construction,
and in other services, we have advanced increasingly
toward public ownership with every decade.

In the past, we as a people have given our main
attention to the problem of increasing the productivity of industry. We have given little thought to
the problem of how best to distribute the fruits of
industry, or to the question of social control. As a
result of this one-sided development, while we now
have an industrial equipment capable of providing a
secure and comfortable living for all, we are at the
same time faced with widespread poverty, tragic
unemployment, and a veritable breakdown of our
economic life. The main task before us is thus the
task of providing that form of social control which
will insure to the plain people of the country the
maximum degree of security and social well-being.
That task requires the hardest kind of thinking and
the most effective kind of political and economic
organization of which we are capable. It is the most
challenging task before all of us today.

CREDIT AS A SOCIAL INSTRUMENT

Harold Reed

CREDIT is usually regarded as an exceedingly abstruse subject. But, however puzzling certain aspects of this commercial instrumentality may be, events of recent years have brought the subject close to the thoughts of every individual in our economic society. During the depression almost all of us have been forcefully reminded that we have debts to discharge, and business men of all classes have been experiencing great difficulty in inducing lenders to let them continue to remain indebted. Creditors have been alert to find out whether the obligations of others to them are really good. They have reduced their credit offerings to debtors; and this pressure on borrowers has been the outstanding feature of the recent business recession. The term "credit" thus means that some one has let somebody else get in debt to him. As there are debtors and creditors, so also are there debts, or debits, and credits on opposite sides of the balance sheets of business operations.

Since every operation of trade must necessarily get someone in debt, if only for the briefest period of time, we may, perhaps, speak of credit as an actor who plays a part in almost every business transaction. One particular type of credit—bank deposits, which are only the promises to pay of a bank—is the customary medium of payment in perhaps 95 per cent of the wholesale trade of the country; and, even in the retail trade, bank credit is employed in upward of 70 per cent of all transactions. Such statistical estimates, moreover, do not begin to tell the whole truth of credit's great importance. By keeping accounts with each other, numerous business men balance obligations and thus avoid, or at least reduce, the need of a medium of payment. Even in the so-called "cash transactions," the characteristics of credit are largely present. Of the money in circulation less than one-fifth is gold, and the remaining four-fifths may be regarded as government promises to pay.

We have personified credit as one of the principal actors in the great drama of business, and as such we must picture him as a very large and portly figure. Nevertheless, when in good health, he is extremely vigorous and active. Each dollar of bank credit annually serves in more than thirty dollars' worth of business transactions. It is no wonder, then, that when this party becomes ill, all other participants on the commercial stage suffer with him and the quality of the performance deteriorates. It is because of credit's key position that statesmen and economists, who have been so greatly concerned with the problem of eliminating the periodic collapses to which our economic system is subject, have devoted major efforts to preserving the health and vigor of this star player.

Despite all the experience of decades, however, our currency physicians either have learned very little about the hygiene of credit, or have failed to secure a hearing among those who direct its use. Since the close of 1929, bank credit has lost more than a tenth of its size and its activity has been reduced about three-tenths. During 1931 the decline in its volume was four times greater than that suffered in 1930, and six times that of 1929. Almost without interruption since the 1929 reaction the number of credit actors, as well as the vigor of each performer, has steadily declined. And all this has occurred during a period in which credit has been sheltered under the most modern of structures, the Federal Reserve system.

To what shall we attribute credit's recent infirmities? Many are the explanations, but in my opinion primary emphasis is to be attached to our failure to perceive that credit cannot be constantly and permanently overworked. If pushed to excessive activity at one time, credit must suffer a relapse on a later occasion. All of this is clearly illustrated by calling attention to developments prior to the 1929 reaction.

For no prolonged period of time in the half-dozen years or so preceding 1929 had there been any pronounced tendency for commodity price averages to advance, and during these years as a whole there was no unusual growth in the total outstanding supply of bank credit. Under these conditions it was somewhat difficult to detect evidences of inflation.

What we did not see then, as clearly as we do now, was the fact that the mere advance in security prices was releasing a lot of credit for business use that otherwise would have been sluggishly employed, so that business men were able to use a much larger amount of credit than seemed to be reported by figures of bank deposits, or of bank loans and investments. We did not then seem to understand that any bull market, particularly in securities, induces multitudes of individual bank depositors to exchange their bank credit for securities so that corporations issuing such securities found it relatively easy to obtain funds for actual business use. The credit resources of the country were then so actively employed that, without any great expansion, statistically speaking, in its total supply, credit was extremely abundant for those who had enterprises to finance.

It is curious indeed that at this juncture the Federal Reserve Board was proclaiming that speculative activity was making credit unavailable for other uses. Quite the reverse was, in fact, the truth. Many types of industry, particularly factory construction, highway building, and heavy machinery, were profiting temporarily from the excessive *availability* of credit and were being grossly overdone. It would, then, have been far better if the Board's diagnosis had been correct, and security speculation had deprived these industries of credit. But these so-called "heavy industries" were not handicapped by any actual shortage of credit, and thus the enthusiasm of the time enabled them to carry on to a point wherein difficulty was inevitably experienced in finding a market for their products.

It is today perfectly clear that what we most needed to know before the 1929 reaction was that the stock-market advance could not go on forever, and that, when it should recede, much of the existing supply of credit would become unavailable for actual use. It was necessary for us to realize that bull-market conditions must, in the course of time, be reversed, and that, in a bear market, bank credit cannot be normally active.

When security prices are falling there is a general tendency among bank depositors to refrain from using their credit in normal degree until the point is reached where there is confidence that the low point has arrived. The refusal of depositors to use their bank credit normally, a phenomenon somewhat similar in its effects to the actual hoarding of currency, is the inevitable consequence of every bear market in securities and capital values. And in every such recession, the story of credit contraction is not sufficiently told by showing the reduction in the outstanding *supply* of credit. Account must also be taken of its subnormal *activity*.

If credit is to be compelled to function as an efficient instrument of social welfare, therefore, attention must be devoted to its activity as well as to its total supply. But at this point it will be objected that we have no effective agency for regulating credit's activity. In our type of economic organization it cannot be expected that any permanent bureau can be set up for the purpose of advising investors when the time has come to put their credit to work by purchasing securities; or when they should insist on keeping their moneyed wealth idle by preserving bank accounts. Credit works, in other words, when the public insists, but in the absence of compulsion is inclined to value its leisure. Shall we then conclude that, while we may organize our banking system to exercize some influence upon the size of our credit supply, we can do little to control credit's activity?

Were it not for one fact it might be necessary to answer the question with a hopeless affirmative and consign our inquiry to the realm of insolvable problems. But the evidence seems to show that the supply of credit is one of the important factors determining the conditions which incite credit to excessive, or to deficient, activity. When, at a time of reviving confidence, business is permitted to feed on any considerable, even though temporary, enlargement in the credit supply, conditions tend to develop which increase the inclination of the public to put idle funds to work.

Thus it is plausible to assume that the rapid credit expansion late in 1924 paved the way for the investment boom of 1925, and that the increased accessibility of credit in 1927 helped to stimulate the almost uncontrollable speculation of 1928 and 1929.

On the other hand, it may also be true that the failure of our banking system to avoid rapid contraction of the credit supply in 1930 and 1931 was largely responsible for the development of conditions which have led bank depositors to refrain from making normal use of their bank accounts in the purchase either of goods or of securities.

Analysis of our financial experience in recent years thus seems to indicate that a policy of confining the growth of credit to an annual rate somewhat similar to that of the estimated long-term increase in the physical volume of trade would have gone far to reduce the intensity of the present liquidation.

If, in addition to such a policy, our central banking authorities had understood the expansive influence of rising security prices and had insisted during the bull market upon a somewhat lesser rate of credit growth than is assumed to be necessary over the course of years, the excessive volume of debts under which industry is now staggering might have been confined within reasonable bounds. If debts had been thus restricted, particular industries could not have engaged in such ambitious extensions, the economic system would not be so unbalanced, and there would be a more fertile field in which the seeds of credit expansion might now be sown.

But as things are it has proved difficult, if not impossible, for our central banking system during the present depression to create such money-market conditions as are necessary to induce sound borrowers to employ more credit. To the absolute contraction in the supply of credit, there has been joined the devastating influence of subnormal activity. The recent hoarding of currency is also to be regarded as the inevitable offspring of an idle-credit father.

The important lessons of the recent past thus seem to be that, in years of prosperity and confidence when credit is actively employed, every endeavor should be made to avoid rapid increase in the outstanding supply of credit; while, in years of impaired confidence, subnormal use of credit should be counteracted by enlarging the available supply. When the soldiers at the front are weary and harried the time has come to summon the reserves and for this purpose a mobile army of reserves should be maintained.

THE DEPRESSION AND THE
WORLD-COMMUNITY

FELIX MORLEY

YOU have been listening, during successive Saturday evenings at this hour, to a series of addresses in which various phases of the current economic depression have been discussed by experts. It is this diagnosis by trained economists, with no ax to grind and no panacea to advocate, which has been the outstanding feature in this novel use of the radio, and which accounts for the nation-wide interest these addresses have aroused. And now that our program has reached its close it is appropriate for us to consider whether any lesson remains outstanding as a result of these broadcasts, and what theme can be detected as common to discussions which, superficially, have treated of very different problems.

I think it is unquestionable that the basis from which all of our speakers have approached their various subjects is definable as the interdependence of modern society. This has been true in such seemingly diverse addresses as those on agricultural problems, on wage and banking policies, on social insurance, and on credit. The same underlying theme, of course, has been much more apparent in such subjects as that of economic planning, to which six talks were devoted early this year. The very word "planning" carries the inference of a society so integrated and bound together that a program for the solution of its problems can be worked out. And the growth of the idea of planning is only one of many indications at hand to show that our society has reached the stage where it is not only possible but even essential that we should plan.

Behind the increasing interdependence of modern life we find two factors, which might as accurately be called two results of the marvelous scientific advance which is the outstanding characteristic of our age. One is the geographic shrinkage of the world in which we live, which is rapidly making the most distant communities as truly our neighbors as were those in an adjacent state a century ago. Side by side with this shrinkage has come an economic expansion which today binds our individual and corporate well-being with those of peoples who may at first glance seem alien or even antagonistic. A simple illustration will serve to point the change that has taken place. Fifteen years ago, at a time when many still thought that the world could be divided into isolated communities with opposing interests, we in this country were hoping to see a complete collapse of Germany. Last summer, when post-war experience had begun to teach us more of the interdependence of modern life, everyone, in a position to know the facts, was praying that a financial and economic collapse in Germany might be averted. This we hoped not so much out of sympathy for the Germans, but because we could feel our own financial fabric shaking in response to the tremors which threatened disaster across the Atlantic.

If we should, tomorrow, drive out to a nearby airport and there witness mechanics endeavoring to repair an airplane with tools which sufficed for making an ox-cart in the eighteenth century, we would be both amused and puzzled by the spectacle. Yet all around us, today, are more striking incongruities which we pass unnoticed. Perhaps the most fundamental is the way in which we are trying to run an economic system which has become thoroughly international on the basis of a parochial nationalism.

Our economic system, known as capitalism, is one which in the past few decades has developed along thoroughly international lines. The arterial lifeflow of this system, whether we consider it from the viewpoint of finance, commerce, or credit, is world-wide in its circulation. The veins may be national but the arteries are international. Yet, under the mistaken assumption that we still live in an age which is past, we allow ourselves to impede and block the arterial flow of our economic system with such artificial obstructions as tariffs, trade embargoes, crushingly unproductive armament expenditures, and many other restrictions to the cooperative life which the capitalist system demands.

This lack of balance between our international economic organization on the one hand and our national political psychology on the other hand, has reached a stage of opposition where one or the other must give way. So far it is the nationalistic attitude which has triumphed, but only at the expense of an injury to our economic system so grave that there are some who are beginning to doubt its recuperative powers. This dislocation of our present economic order is fundamentally a result of trying to handle a highly complicated organization with primitive and out-of-date ideas. The attempt is no less ironical than would be an effort to build a flying machine with pine boards, hammer, and saw. But, where such a pastime would merely be ludicrous, to attempt to run a twentieth-century economic system by eighteenth-century political ideas is almost suicidal.

Behind this conflict between national political organization and international economic and financial organization lies a theory which must shortly be reinterpreted in the light of actual facts. This theory is that of national sovereignty, with its implications that each state shall be the sole judge of its own policies in the international field, without regard to whether those policies prove immediately disastrous to other peoples and ultimately disastrous to those who launch them. We have seen great changes in the theory of sovereignty in this country since the days when thirteen sovereign, free, and independent states combined to form the nucleus of our federal union. Today it would be regarded as intolerable if one of our sovereign states should erect tariff barriers and otherwise attempt to isolate itself from the remainder of the American community. For the well-being of our civilization and the international economic system on which it rests the present situation of national ill will and hostility is just as intolerable. We are too prone to ignore the fact that the entire world is today much more of an economic unit than was the United States in 1788. The Pennsylvanian of that day could get along as well without cotton from Georgia as can the Pennsylvanian today get along without rubber from the Malay States.

The idea of sovereignty is confused in the minds of most people with the idea of autonomy. That every community should have the greatest possible autonomy in matters of local concern is a political principle which scarcely needs emphasis. But that it should assert a sovereignty of the sort definable as a complete indifference to the welfare of others is equally unthinkable. It is not unthinkable on ethical grounds, although these are, perhaps, a factor in the argument. It is unthinkable because the welfare of each unit in the modern world is indisseverably linked with others, so that unintelligent insistence on a sovereign attitude reacts in the long run disastrously on those who uphold it. We have an excellent illustration of this vicious circle in the recent news that some of the political leaders of Latin America are endeavoring to establish a virtual continental embargo on our products in retaliation against our mounting duties on their exports to us.

Quicker than most of us realize, such policies can reduce our standard of living to an almost primitive level.

Very fortunately, many of us are now beginning to see that true sovereignty is something quite different from the interpretation given by some who have nominated themselves as our leading patriots. We have come to realize that an extension of the powers of the community exercising sovereignty need not involve a contraction of the powers of others. That a steamship company operating between Boston and Baltimore has its head offices in New York does not mean that the state of New York is unduly trespassing on the sovereignty of the states of Massachusetts and Maryland. It does mean that for purely natural reasons certain powers have become concentrated in the city of New York which, projected from that community, add to the well-being and prosperity of individuals in several cities.

Instances of this co-operative use of sovereignty are not lacking in the international sphere. Only sixty years ago the old-fashioned conception of national rights almost prevented citizens of one country from having any communication with citizens of others. If an American wished to send a letter to Australia, he would have to send it marked by a certain steamer, paying postage reaching as much as a dollar per half-ounce, according to the route which he selected. With the coming of the International Postal Union all this has been changed. Each nation has voluntarily limited its sovereign right to control the entry of letters from foreign countries in order to secure better facilities for the letters which its citizens send abroad.

The gain can be pictured mathematically. Since there are some sixty independent nations, a certain limitation on our right to control incoming foreign mail has resulted in securing rights from some fifty-nine other countries for our outgoing foreign mail. Here is a clear case in which a seeming limitation of sovereignty has resulted in an actual expansion of that quality. And it would put us more in touch with the facts of our civilization if we would remember that the postman who delivers a foreign letter at our door is at that moment serving in the capacity of an international rather than a national official.

The different governments in the world are obviously, though slowly, coming to the conclusion that each is more competent to further the well-being of its citizens—and that is the only objective for which a government exists—by co-operating with other governments. As a result of this tendency we have such movements as the Pan-American Union, the idea of a European federation, the voluntary manner in which the British Empire continues to hang together, and, most important of all, the League of Nations. In this bicentennial year it is highly appropriate to recall that George Washington, who is falsely called a prophet of national isolation, anticipated and approved such co-operation on the part of this country. In his own words he anticipated a time when "our institutions being firmly consolidated and working with complete success, we might safely and perhaps beneficially take part in the consultations held by foreign States for the advantage of the nations." In the eighteenth century such an attitude on the part of an American was very farsighted. In the twentieth century any other attitude on the part of an American is very shortsighted.

It is clear, however, that intergovernmental co-operation is not enough to adjust our political situation to the facts of the world-community which has arisen with the passing of the sailing ship and the pony express. Authority of the officials of a government is necessarily limited by a political frontier which means much less in the fields of science, the arts, commerce, industry, and finance. The frontier has a reality for officialdom which it lacks for those, wherever they are, who are engaged in kindred occupations. It is on the assumption of the unity of working-class interests, entirely regardless of geographical location, that the communist philosophy is built. The man who denies a certain philosophic validity to this idea is painfully ignorant of the strength of the communist doctrine and therefore woefully incompetent to cope with it. The more intelligent course today is to recognize that there is real value in international functional co-operation, but that this value is not limited to unity of those who wish to see the establishment of a cruder social order. It is plain that nationality

means very little in a congress of chemists or physicists drawn from many countries. Since the chemists
and physicists are determining the character of the
world in which we live it is certainly advisable to
consider the implications of their ability to co-
operate.

The growing tendency toward occupational co-
operation, side by side with that of governmental
co-operation, is obvious when once we look for
it. In 1927 there was summoned at Geneva a great
World Economic Conference, representative of banking, industrial, commercial, co-operative, labor, and
consuming groups. The work of that conference
has been largely dissipated by the depression, already on its way when the conference met. For the
depression has led to further efforts to solve international problems through such nationalistic tactics
as higher tariffs and further trade restrictions, each
of which has, of course, rendered the effects of the
depression worse. The fact that this conference of
1927 proved relatively unsuccessful does not, however, mean that there was anything wrong with its
theory. We shall, undoubtedly, have more and
more of such conferences in the future. Our Congress, for instance, has recently requested that one be
called. For such conferences, and the occupational
co-operation which will be learned from them, point
a permanent way out of such difficulties as now
beset us.

It is not easy to discern the real significance of
current history as mankind writes his record on the

unfolding page. But one would be blind not to appreciate the vital importance of the increasing network of international contacts which in recent years have bound the world into a single economic community. At first the only international political contacts were between the foreign offices of the different countries, a contact which may be represented by placing the index fingers of your two hands together. Since the war contacts between foreign ministries have been augmented by intergovernmental contacts of many types, such as between departments of commerce in different countries, or such as is represented by the great intergovernmental Disarmament Conference now in progress at Geneva. Such contacts are like an interlocking of all the fingers of your two hands, and their systematic development has been the outstanding contribution of the League of Nations.

Side by side with this growth of intergovernmental contacts, however, there is going on, without much publicity, and in the face of a blatant nationalism which makes the task more difficult, an interlocking of occupational contacts between scientists, industrialists, bankers, rotarians, and chambers of commerce—to mention only a few instances—which will in time help to secure for the world a co-operative political method in balance with the facts of economic life. These contacts may be compared to the interlacing of the nervous system of your entire body. Once established they will provide a unity which will not be broken without dissolution of

that body. Such a unity will provide not merely an
enduring basis for international peace but also a
solid basis now altogether lacking for national
prosperity. It will be a unity which will not sup-
press desirable diversity and it will be thoroughly in
accord with the doctrine of national sovereignty
properly interpreted.

It would be idle to close this series of addresses on
a hollow note of facile cheerfulness. Every economist worthy of the name knows that our civilization, by tearing the international fabric asunder, has
approached a collapse comparable only with the
historic period of social decay which we still rightly call the "Dark Ages," and which lasted not for a
few months or years but for seven or eight centuries.
Every economist knows, however, that there is today no reason for such a collapse unless we ourselves
will it. Therefore the general note of qualified
optimism in the talks to which you have been
listening.

Mankind, in spite of plentiful evidence to the
contrary, is endowed with reasoning powers. There
are hopeful signs that he is using these powers to
build co-operatively amid the present chaos in the
world-community. As Shakespeare makes one of
his characters say in the darkest moment of a
desperate combat:

> "This battle fares like to the morning's war,
>   when dying clouds contend with growing light."

BIBLIOGRAPHY

SUGGESTED READINGS

I. FOR BEGINNING READERS

Calkins, Clinch, *Some Folks Won't Work*. Harcourt, 1930. $1.50.

Carver, T. N., *Principles of Political Economy*. Ginn, 1919. $1.50.

Chase, Stuart, *Men and Machines*. Macmillan, 1930. College edition, $1.75.

Clay, Henry, *Economics, An Introduction for the General Reader*. Macmillan, 1918. $2.50.

Hayward, W. R., and Johnson, G. W., *Story of Man's Work*. Minton, 1925. $2.00.

Johnson, Alvin, *Introduction to Economics* (revised and enlarged edition). Heath, 1922. $2.40.

Lynd, R. S., and H. M., *Middletown, A Study in Contemporary American Culture*. Harcourt, 1929. $5.00.

Marshall, L. C., and Lyon, L. S., *Our Economic Organization*. Macmillan, 1921. $1.68.

Pollak, K. M., and Tippet, Tom, *Your Job and Your Pay*. Vanguard, 1931. $2.00.

Slichter, Sumner H., *Modern Economic Society*. Holt, 1931. $5.00.

Soule, George H., Jr., *The Useful Art of Economics*. Macmillan, 1929. $2.00.

Thorp, Willard, *Economic Institutions* ("World Today Bookshelf"). Macmillan, 1928. $1.50.

II. BOOKS ON SOME SPECIAL ASPECTS OF ECONOMIC LIFE FOR BEGINNERS

Black, J. D. and A. G., *Introduction to Production Economics*. Holt, 1926. $4.50.

Chase, Stuart, and Schlink, F. J., *Your Money's Worth*. Macmillan, 1927. $1.00.

Donham, Wallace B., *Business Adrift*. McGraw-Hill, 1931. $2.50.

Douglas, P. H., and Director, Aaron, *The Problem of Unemployment*. Macmillan, 1931. $3.50.

Filene, Edward A., and Wood, Charles W., *Successful Living in This Machine Age*. Simon and Schuster, 1931. $2.50.

Harper, Elsie D., *Out of a Job*. Woman's Press, 1931. $0.50.

Laidler, H. W., *Unemployment and Its Remedies*. League for Industrial Democracy, 1930. $0.15.

Lorwin, Lewis L., *Labor and Internationalism*. Brookings Institution, 1929. $3.00.

Lyon, L. S., *Making a Living*. Macmillan, 1926. $1.60.

Moulton, H. G., *The Financial Organization of Society* (third edition). University of Chicago Press, 1930. $4.00.

Patterson, E. M., *The World's Economic Dilemma*. McGraw-Hill, 1930. $3.50.

Tugwell, R. G., *Industry's Coming of Age*. Harcourt, 1927. $2.00.

BIBLIOGRAPHY

Tugwell, R. G., Munro, Thomas, and Stryker, R. E., *American Economic Life* (third edition). Harcourt, 1930. $4.00.

Wallace, Benjamin B., and Edminster, Lynn R., *International Control of Raw Materials*. Brookings Institution, 1930. $3.50.

III. More Advanced General Works in Economics

Bogart, Ernest L., *Economic History of the American People*. Longmans, Green, 1931. $3.50.

Bye, R. T., and Hewett, W. W., *Applied Economics*. Knopf, 1928. $3.75.

Davenport, H. J., *The Economics of Enterprise*. Macmillan, 1913. $3.25.

Edie, Lionel D., *Economics, Principles and Programs*. Crowell, 1926. $5.00.

Marshall, Alfred, *Principles of Economics* (eighth edition). Macmillan, 1920. $6.00.

Taussig, F. W., *Principles of Economics* (third edition). Macmillan, 1921. 2 vols., $3.00 each.

Taylor, Horace, *Making Goods and Making Money*. Macmillan, 1928. $2.50.

IV. More Advanced Special Works in Economics

Angell, J. W., *The Recovery of Germany*. Yale University Press, 1929. $4.00.

Black, John D., *Agricultural Reform in the United States*. McGraw-Hill, 1929. $4.00.

Dewey, Davis R., *Financial History of the United States* (eighth edition). Longmans, Green, 1922. $3.75, text edition $3.00.

Douglas, Paul H., *Real Wages in the United States*. Houghton, 1930. $7.50.

Edie, L. D., *Capital, the Money Market, and Gold*. University of Chicago Press, 1929. $0.50.

Ely, Richard T., *Elements of Land Economics*. Macmillan, 1924. $3.50.

Feis, Herbert, *Europe the World's Banker, 1870–1914*. Yale University Press, 1930. $5.00.

Gay, Edwin F., Mitchell, W. C., and Others, *Recent Economic Changes in the United States*. National Bureau of Economic Research, 1929. McGraw-Hill. 2 vols., $7.50.

Hammond, J. L. and Barbara, *The Rise of Modern Industry*. Harcourt, 1926. $2.75.

Mitchell, W. C., *Business Cycles: The Problem and Its Setting*. National Bureau of Economic Research, 1927. $6.50.

Moulton, H. G., *Germany's Capacity To Pay*. Brookings Institution, 1923. $2.50.

Nourse, E. G., *American Agriculture and the European Market*. Brookings Institution, 1924. $2.50.

Reed, Harold, *Federal Reserve Policy, 1921–1930*. McGraw-Hill, 1930. $2.50

V. Special Collateral Reading for Scheduled Addresses

Atkins, McConnell, Edwards, Raushenbush, Friedrich, and Reed, *Economic Behavior: An Institutional Approach*. Houghton Mifflin, 1931. 2 vols., $8.50; students' edition, $6.00.

NEW SOCIAL RESPONSIBILITIES

Beard, Charles A. (editor), *America Faces the Future*. Houghton Mifflin, 1932. $3.00.

Black, John D., *Agricultural Reform in the United States*. McGraw-Hill, 1929. $4.00.

Carroll, Mollie Ray, *Unemployment Insurance in Germany*. Brookings Institution, 1929. $2.50.

Chamberlin, Wm. H., *The Soviet Planned Economic Order*. World Peace Foundation, 1931. $2.50.

Clark, F. E., *Principles of Marketing*. Macmillan, 1922. $3.00.

Clark, J. M., *Social Control of Business*. University of Chicago Press, 1926. $4.00.

Commons, John R., *Principles of Labor Legislation* (revised edition). Harper, 1927. $3.00.

Counts, George S., *The Soviet Challenge to America*. Day, 1931.

Gray, L. C., and Baker, O. E., *Land Utilization and the Farm Problem*, "Miscellaneous Publication 97." U.S. Department of Agriculture, 1930. $0.25.

Hoover, Calvin B., *The Economic Life of Soviet Russia*. Macmillan, 1931. $3.00.

Keezer, D. M., and May, Stacy, *Public Control of Business*. Harper, 1930. $3.00, texts $2.25.

Laidler, Harry W., *Concentration of Control in American Industry*. Crowell, 1931. $3.75.

Lorwin, Lewis L., *Advisory Economic Councils*. (Pamphlet Series), Brookings Institution, 1932. $0.50.

Nourse, Edwin G., and Knapp, Joseph G., *The Co-operative Marketing of Livestock*. Brookings Institution, 1931. $3.50.

Person, H. S. (editor), *Scientific Management in American Industry*. Harper, 1931. $6.00, text edition $4.00.

Rogers, J. H., *America Weighs Her Gold*. Yale University Press, 1931. $3.00.

Stewart, Bryce, *Unemployment Benefits in the United States*. Industrial Relations Counsellors, 1930. $7.50.

Survey-Graphic, March, 1932. "Economic Planning." $0.30.

Taussig, F. W., *A Tariff History of the United States* (eighth edition). Putnam's, 1931. $3.00.

Wolman, Leo, *Planning and Control of Public Works*. National Bureau of Economic Research, 1930. $3.00.